CW01628938

# The Forgotten Nurses

Finding Peace and Purpose in the Stressful World of Veterinary Medicine

Tracy L. Bittner, LVT

The Forgotten Nurses © Copyright October 2021 Tracy L. Bittner, LVT

All rights reserved. No part of this publication may be reproduced, distributed, or transmitted in any form or by any means, including photocopying, recording, or other electronic or mechanical methods, without the prior written permission of the publisher, except in the case of brief quotations embodied in critical reviews and certain other noncommercial uses permitted by copyright law.

Although the author and publisher have made every effort to ensure that the information in this book was correct at press time, the author and publisher do not assume and hereby disclaim any liability to any party for any loss, damage, or disruption caused by errors or omissions, whether such errors or omissions result from negligence, accident, or any other cause.

The resources in this book are provided for informational purposes only and should not be used to replace the specialized training and professional judgment of a healthcare or mental healthcare professional.

Neither the author nor the publisher can be held responsible for the use of the information provided within this book. Please always consult a trained professional before making any decision regarding treatment of yourself or others.

Adherence to all applicable laws and regulations, including international, federal, state, and local governing professional licensing, business practices, advertising, and all other aspects of doing business in the US, Canada, or any other jurisdiction is the sole responsibility of the reader and consumer.

Neither the author nor the publisher assumes any responsibility or liability whatsoever on behalf of the consumer or reader of this material. Any perceived slight of any individual or organization is purely unintentional. All names have been changed or omitted to protect the innocent (and guilty).

For more information, email silkenmoon129@gmail.com.

ISBN: 978-1-7375917-0-2 (paperback)

ISBN: 978-1-7375917-2-6 (Kindle e-book)

# TABLE OF CONTENTS

# DEDICATION

This book is dedicated to all those who have experienced bullying and burnout in the workplace—those who didn't survive the experience and those willing to make a change in the culture.

# FOREWORD

I have known Tracy Bittner as a colleague and friend for the better part of twenty years. Tracy moved to Richmond for its rich and storied history. I had just opened a new veterinary practice specializing in ophthalmology, and she took a job as an LVT working for me. She was with me for a couple of years before moving to another veterinary practice, but we have remained friends. We have a mutual interest in sighthounds and continue to share stories after all these years. Tracy is the perfect author for this book. Sharing her story will give the reader a deeper perspective of life, particularly in the stressful world of veterinary medicine. By the grace of God, she was able to work through the most difficult issues, and she is here to tell this story.

This book brings to light some of the troubling aspects of life in the veterinary medical field. Yet it brings a message of hope. The work is meant to enlighten people so that they can deal with stressful and fatiguing life situations, whether in the field of veterinary medicine or any other field. Through Tracy's story, the reader will gain an understanding of what it means to be the forgotten nurse. I have personal experience with the tragedy that can occur within the world of veterinary medicine. In the summer of 2013, a beautiful single mom named Sherry with two young children came to work for me as an LVT. We welcomed her into our work family, as we truly treat every employee as a part of our family. She seemed to be very happy. We took her to our annual conference in Puerto Rico, as she worked very hard and was well liked by everyone. Later that year, we could see her struggling with life and the stress of our busy practice, but she never opened up. She took some time off around Christmas, but we were unaware that she was in the hospital due to a deliberate overdose of medication. Over the next six months, she was even more distracted from her work. We never realized how serious things were. Little did we know she would tragically end her life by administering medications she obtained from our hospital. She was found deceased in our office in July of 2014. A horrible tragedy such as this is the reason this book is so important.

In this book, Tracy finds a way to guide the reader through darkness with great lessons and messages. The value of this work is compounded by the current pandemic, which has influenced all of us and weighed heavily on veterinary practices everywhere. I am sure you will find this story intriguing, happy, sad, compassionate, and fulfilling, but most of all, very possibly life-saving.

Sincerely,

Michael J. Blair, DVM MS RPh

Diplomate American College of Veterinary Ophthalmologists

# PREFACE: THE SHADOW SIDE OF VETERINARY MEDICINE

Unless you're an active member of the veterinary medicine community, you are probably unaware that there is a mental health crisis within the industry. This doesn't mean we're all crazy; it means we are under a whole lot of stress for a multitude of reasons. If we don't learn how to deal with the stress, the risks can be enormous. The suicide rate in veterinary medicine is up to 3.5 times higher than that in the general population. It is currently reported that one in six veterinarians has considered taking their own life. For those who are serious, the act is almost always completed. We have discussions with clients weekly, if not daily, about how euthanasia ends suffering. It's not a far leap to conclude that veterinarians and licensed technicians are adept at administering the life-ending drugs they have access to. Almost everyone outside the industry is shocked by this information. Clients see us put on a happy face and have no idea what goes on beyond the exam room door. Many of them think we play with puppies and kittens all day and get paid well for it. Those of us in the business know that this public fantasy is far from reality. So what is the truth? This book will shed some light on the darker aspects of the veterinary industry, illuminate the shadows of mental health, and hopefully start to change the culture to one of health and wellness.

Veterinarians deal with what feels like insurmountable debt coming out of school, with wages that are half those of their human healthcare counterparts upon graduation. This means it takes them twice as long to pay off their student loan debt. Licensed veterinary technicians make one-half to one-third the salary of registered nurses. Like human doctors and nurses, we suffer from long hours with few, if any, breaks during a workday, which leaves us mentally and physically exhausted. On top of this, we have to know the needs of and differences between multiple species, none of which speak our language, which can be both intriguing and frustrating. No matter what we ultimately choose to specialize in, we have to at least know the basics about dogs, cats, horses, cows, goats, pigs, rabbits, ferrets, rats, geckos, snakes, iguanas, birds . . . you get the point. Each species has different husbandry, nutritional, and medical requirements. Many of these animals can be fearful or downright aggressive, which can lead to disfiguring or career-ending bites or kicks. Assistants and technicians are constantly covered in bruises, scratches, and bites. One of my friends was handed a domestic abuse hotline card every time she went to a nearby gas station, no matter how many times she tried to convince the owner that it was animals that were beating her up. This situation has gotten worse, especially during the pandemic, when owners either couldn't or wouldn't socialize and train their dogs. They find it amusing when their eighty-five-pound Doodle jumps all over the staff and drags them around on the end of their long retractable leash. You have to have quick reflexes and always be alert and aware to survive in this profession.

Dealing with a pet's caretakers can be frustrating. Most are wonderful and supportive, but too many are difficult on numerous levels, ranging from unrealistic expectations for care to arguments over finances. Our prices don't hold a candle to the cost of human healthcare. How often have we heard, "After all I've spent here, I've probably put a new wing on this building!" (Sorry, but that wing cost more than the $450 you spend here annually.) Clients vilify veterinarians for not being able to cure their pets when they don't want to spend the money for diagnostics, then take to social media for a smear campaign. They have no idea what is going on in the back of the clinic. Often we are dealing with circumstances beyond our control such as triaging emergencies or falling behind schedule due to late clients. As an industry, we have failed to establish boundaries, and all too often we accommodate unpleasant clientele. We leave medications in the mailbox so clients can pick them up after-hours, we drive medications or pet food to their homes, and we bend over backward to fit them into an already-full schedule when they insist that we do so. We have created our own monster, and it's only getting worse as the general public becomes increasingly entitled and demanding. As a population we have a "microwave mentality," where everything needs to be done *right now* or else cursing, other abusive language, and threats ensue. We should have a zero tolerance policy for treating staff members with disrespect.

Veterinarians and technicians can battle what's called *impostor syndrome*, a condition in which we silently question whether we know what we're doing and if we are doing our best with every case. We can feel like frauds, even after all our years of education. We may get out of school having learned all the latest and greatest techniques and equipment, only to find that our new boss is still practicing in the dark ages. As I've mentioned, we have access to controlled drugs, many of which are highly addictive or fatal if misused. There have now been many corporate takeovers of the mom-and-pop-type vet clinics, which brings a whole new level of stress, with non-medical upper management focused on bringing in the money. At some corporate-owned hospitals, veterinarians may not be allowed the freedom to practice as they wish but instead must adhere to strict protocols. Big-box stores and online pharmacies have taken over many of our steady streams of revenue, from prescription medications to low-cost spays and neuters. Pet owners either don't know or don't care that by saving a few dollars, they are taking income away from the very people who truly care about their pet's health.

Veterinary staff can also suffer from *compassion fatigue* and caregiver burnout. Compassion fatigue (also known as secondary traumatic stress or secondary victimization) is a real issue that medical staff deal with, and it takes a toll on many of us. Some of the signs of compassion fatigue are pent-up emotions, feeling drained mentally and physically, difficulty concentrating, physical ailments, flashbacks or nightmares, substance abuse, complaining, and sadness or depression. Due to the empathy we feel for our patients, we take on a huge emotional burden when they are sick or dying, which veterinary staff have the unique situation of dealing with on a daily basis. One day I helped humanely euthanize seven patients—the seventh was my own dog, who was suffering from end-stage kidney disease. Sometimes being strong takes a toll. Add to this the ethical and moral dilemmas that veterinarians face when treating or euthanizing pets for clients who have a subpar level of compassion or limited funds, and you can maybe start to understand why we have such a high incidence of stress-related health issues. We put on a brave face, then cry alone. Many people numb themselves with drugs or alcohol, although they know that won't make the problems go away. Not dealing with your emotions doesn't solve anything. It just prolongs the inevitable, and eventually it catches up to you. Suffering in silence when you have no control over a situation isn't healthy. Be aware of what you're thinking and feeling and find ways to work through it. Do not hesitate to get professional help if you need it.

In addition to all of this external stress is something I have a lot of personal experience with: internal workplace bullying and gaslighting (where your perception and judgment are questioned and invalidated, causing fear, anxiety, self-doubt, and inner turmoil). I discuss this in more detail in a later chapter. These difficulties are compounded by the fact that this is a passion-driven profession, with sensitive and caring individuals who have high levels of empathy and compassion. So many vets work after-hours or on weekends, researching cases to provide the best medical options. I wish more clients knew how much their animals mean to us instead of calling us money-hungry and uncaring. I vividly remember pets from decades ago and still think of them. I have personally buried ashes of patients in my own garden when it's a pet I have a deep connection with. We have big hearts, with a tendency to want to fix, heal, and rescue, which can leave us vulnerable to bullies who like to prey on those they *perceive* as weak. Even though being kind and empathetic does not mean we *are* weak, we can quickly lose our way, becoming disgruntled with the profession that once sounded like a dream career. A friend of mine described her relationship with veterinary medicine as "abusive—it beats the crap out of you physically and emotionally, but you can't stop coming back to it." Many people won't know or understand what we go through if we don't speak up. Mental health and stress aren't real to some people because they aren't always tangible. So we soldier on and suffer in silence. Let's all do our part to make our profession less abusive and more enjoyable. This book will give you the tools to combat stress leading to burnout and reignite your passion for the profession, so you can face your days with confidence and purpose. Don't let your outer circumstances determine your emotional well-being.

# CHAPTER 1:
# THE FORGOTTEN NURSES

When the COVID-19 pandemic hit, none of us could have predicted the giant boom in our profession. At first we were all afraid we'd be shut down and lose our source of income. Instead, we were inundated with new clients and patients when many people suddenly found themselves at home and decided it was a great time to buy a puppy or kitten. According to an American Veterinary Medical Association (AVMA) survey, there was a 70% increase in people inquiring about pet adoption during the pandemic! Even if only a small percentage of them actually adopted, most clinics weren't equipped to handle the sudden influx, especially because there was already a shortage of licensed techs and other qualified staff. Since 2018, the US pet population has increased by 48 million, yet only 5,320 new veterinarians have been added. That translates to approximately one doctor for every 2200 cats and dogs (and that's only considering small animals). In addition, since people were working from home, they were noticing more issues with their existing pets and making appointments for them. Daytime clinic waiting room times nearly doubled, and many emergency hospitals had wait times as long as several hours with limited staff. The veterinary profession also scrambled to navigate the "new normal" of not allowing clients into the building.

Overnight, we had to figure out how to best serve our clientele while they waited in their cars. This was understandably stressful for both owners and their pets.

Assistants and technicians were in and out of the clinic multiple times a day for a year, no matter the weather. Oftentimes we were sweating, freezing, or slogging through a downpour. We tried our best to gather up nervous and confused pets while avoiding contact with their owners. Some clients would immediately jump out of their cars as soon as they saw us coming and hand over their animal before we could ask any questions about their visit. To others we were completely invisible, standing at their car window while they texted away in oblivion. Some refused to bring their sick pets to us unless they were allowed in the building, then blamed the staff for their pet not getting treated. Many people would pull down their masks while talking to you, then pull them back up when listening. A few clients broke their active COVID quarantine to bring their "fur baby" to the doctor, knowingly putting the staff at risk. As animal caregivers, we take precautions to protect ourselves against zoonotic infections that can be passed from animals to humans: rabies, leptospirosis, ringworm, intestinal parasites, etc., but no one predicted a human-to-human deadly disease. I am blessed that everyone I know personally has so far come out of this basically unscathed—things could have been much worse.

As caseloads for veterinarians dramatically increased, clients became more frustrated and demanding, overwhelming an already exhausted and limited team. During the pandemic, veterinary hospital staff were considered essential personnel and were allowed to remain working. For that we were grateful, but it came with significant risks. We had to pivot quickly to deal with the unique challenges of our profession. Although we were essential workers, there was a global shortage of protective gear. Most of it was diverted to struggling human healthcare facilities, which understandably had a more immediate need. Vet clinics could barely get masks and gloves, let alone any other PPE. We tried to maintain social distancing, but there's only so far away we can be from each other or clients when handling animals. Drawing blood on a pet while six feet away from your assistant who's holding it just isn't possible. We had to weigh what was more important: putting ourselves and our families at risk to help the animals who depend on us or not going to work to try to stay safe. Everyone I know personally was committed to working, but there were certainly many who quit altogether. Our bosses had to make decisions about which surgeries and procedures were considered essential for pets, to limit contact with their owners. Many hospitals stopped doing routine wellness visits and surgeries such as spays and neuters and concentrated only on emergencies. Most clinics allowed clients in the building only to be with their pets in their last moments during a euthanasia.

In time, the pandemic knocked on almost all of our doors, and many vet hospitals had to close down or operate with limited staff until everyone recovered. Most clients understood this, although some were demanding, entitled, and impatient. We've been yelled at, cursed at, and given bad reviews. People had no concept of what we were going through behind the scenes to try to accommodate everyone in a timely fashion. *Yes, you need to wear a mask. No, we are not allowing people in the building. We're so sorry you had to wait fifteen minutes for your dog's vaccines, but the staff was trying desperately to save a dog that was hit by a car or preparing a pet for emergency bloat surgery.* As I mentioned earlier, our profession needs to get very clear on what we are willing to tolerate—there has to be respectful two-way communication.

Of course, there were many moments of humor as well when dealing with curbside-only service. It was a bit shocking to all of us that many people have no idea what type of car they drive. *A "Honda Jeep" is not a make of car. No, your truck is not gold; it is metallic silver. What do you mean, you're parked in space 2½? (This isn't Harry Potter's Animal Clinic.) Parking wherever you please does not give you permission to create your own parking space. Just because you forgot your phone doesn't mean you can come into the clinic. Whining, complaining, and threatening won't get you seen any faster!* One couple showed up demanding vaccines—we incorrectly assumed they meant for their pet. Nope, it was COVID vaccines for themselves, and they got angry when we explained that this was a veterinary clinic. They kept insisting that their GPS sent them to *our* clinic. You truly can't make this stuff up. Some clients suddenly found themselves with a limited income, yet their beloved pets still needed medical care. This obviously puts tremendous stress on everyone involved—balancing animal welfare with the caretaker's financial situation to find the best solution. It is sometimes a heartbreaking outcome for all involved and often taxes our morals and values.

Tragically, there were those who took their own lives during that incredibly stressful time. Some made national news and shed light on the issue of suicide and mental health. Sadly, this is nothing new in the veterinary profession, but COVID certainly increased the overwhelming stress of all the other issues we already struggle with. It is time for these issues to be brought into the open and discussed. My idea for this book came amid the height of this struggle.

I was driving home after an especially arduous day, so exhausted I could barely keep my eyes open. I drove past one of our local human hospitals and noticed the giant red-white-and-blue sign that read *Heroes Work Here!* While this is absolutely true, and I'm not taking any accolades away from human doctors and nurses (especially those who dealt with COVID patients), my immediate thought was that all of my veterinary colleagues were heroes as well, every day. Our profession certainly had more than our normal share of daily stress and uncertainty. I felt like our industry was invisible, and the term *the forgotten nurses* came to my mind. I went home and wrote a bunch of my thoughts in a notebook, and this gave me renewed energy and passion. While listening to a podcast, I heard the magic words *"You are most powerfully positioned to serve the person you once were."* I thought of how far I've come since my start in veterinary medicine, both personally and professionally, and how I could share my journey with others. *"One day you will tell your story of how you've overcome what you are going through, and it will become part of someone's survival guide" (tinybuddha.com).*

A huge struggle that licensed veterinary technicians have long faced is the right to be called *veterinary nurses*. This movement is called the Veterinary Nurse Initiative, headed by the National Association of Veterinary Technicians in America (NAVTA). According to the American Nurses Association (ANA), granting us that title could lessen the respect given to human nurses. For over one hundred years, human nurses have fought hard for credibility. Their profession has been voted by a Gallup poll as the most ethical and honest. The ANA has suggested that veterinary technicians want to "co-opt another profession's title to garner respect," as well as saying, "It's irresponsible for another profession to hijack [their title]," "confuse the public," and "undermine" all their hard work in the healthcare industry (www.DVM360.com). I'm fairly certain I won't mislead the general public by calling myself a veterinary nurse. I doubt they're going to point to their child and say, "Oh good, because little Johnny has been coughing for a week." Recently, I am starting to see a noticeable shift within the industry, as drug companies and prescription diet companies are calling us veterinary nurses in their continuing education campaigns. Both physicians and veterinarians are called doctors, so I don't see the issue with us being called nurses. Not all of my peers agree, but I've personally never liked the term *technician*, as it sounds like a job based only on science or technology, instead of enveloping the scope of all we do, including the emotional investment in the care of our patients. I find this endlessly frustrating, as veterinary technicians are also college-educated, take national and state board exams, and have to earn yearly continuing education credits to maintain their licensure, just like registered nurses. Both professions take an oath to care for others—our patients just happen to have fur, fins, or feathers. Most people consider their pets important members of the family. I see human nurses and animal nurses as two sides of the same coin, but the debate continues.

Just like veterinarians, technicians are well-versed in numerous species of animals. In the human medical realm, nurses are typically assigned to specific departments, whereas licensed vet technicians are responsible for a multitude of areas: we are phlebotomists, x-ray technicians, lab technicians, surgery assistants, dental hygienists, and ultrasonographers. We are pharmacy technicians, grief counselors, kitten snugglers, keepers of controlled drug logs, nutritional consultants, copy machine repair people, janitors, morticians, psychologists to angry or distraught clients . . . you get the idea. We usually wear most of these hats in a single day. The only things we can't legally do are diagnose, perform surgery, and prescribe medications. We see the gamut from newborns during a C-section to geriatrics who deserve a dignified end to their suffering. I'm willing to bet that your pediatrician isn't the same person who will provide your hospice care. Yet vets and technicians deal with such emotional highs and lows every week, sometimes within minutes of each other.

I do agree, however, that our industry needs to get its act together and have a standardized title and qualifications. Currently, there are LVTs (licensed veterinary technicians), RVTs (registered veterinary technicians), and CVTs (certified veterinary technicians), depending on which state you are licensed in. In fact, some states allow you to work as a technician without having any education or license, which further devalues the job. It doesn't help matters that we are often not given the respect we deserve by our own bosses and managers, which then trickles down to the rest of the staff. Technician and assistant are often used interchangeably by both clients and staff, which can be confusing to the general public. I once worked at a clinic where the assistant was called a "veterinary technician" (without the *licensed* in front). When I brought this to the manager's attention, I was told, "She wants to be a vet tech." *What?* I told her I wanted to be a veterinarian, so please preemptively add DVM after my name! Many vet techs aren't allowed to utilize their full skill set, which can lead to disenchantment with the profession and decreased morale. Instead of utilizing our professional skills and being treated as the veterinarian's right hand in managing cases, we are more often than not treated like servants. More than half of all vet techs burn out and leave the profession within five years, which is causing a huge strain on an already overwhelmed industry. Their average salary is close to the poverty level in many states, despite a recent AVMA study demonstrating that each licensed technician brings in about a $90,000 annual increase in revenue. An RN friend of mine finished nursing school a year ago; she already makes substantially more than I do after decades in the industry. Many assistants and technicians hold second jobs just to make ends meet. I personally wake up before 5:00 a.m. many days to pet sit before work, and I often don't get home until 9:00 p.m. if I have several to visit after work. While I enjoy what I do, it makes for a very long day.

Veterinarians struggle to keep up with the pace of all their cases and often stay at work well after the clinic has closed to catch up on phone calls and enter their notes into the computer. Doing emergency work is especially stressful, even without clients cursing at you all night. You witness so much death and feel hopeless when clients can't afford to care for their pets. This is especially true around the holidays, which makes it even more heart-wrenching. One technician friend who works in an emergency clinic had to leave her twelve-hour shift with forty-two sick or injured animals needing help and only four people on staff. Several were out on medical leave for mental health issues, and many others had quit altogether. How do you go home and get a good night's rest knowing that you're desperately needed, but you must have time to recover as well? Equine and farm animal vets seem to be on call more often than not, and they have to deal with tragedies not seen in small-animal medicine. If you've ever witnessed a 1200-pound animal thrashing around in pain, you know it's not for the faint of heart. No matter which branch of vet medicine you practice in, you most likely feel overworked, underpaid, and barely appreciated. You may start looking for a way out of your job in particular, the profession in general, or even your life overall. I know. I've been there. But there is hope on the horizon. There are better ways to deal with your stress before it becomes a mental health crisis. One small tweak I've made to my mindset is to say, "I *get* to go to work today" instead of "I *have* to go to work today." This shows gratitude for the privilege of having a job, because not everyone is so lucky to be doing what we dreamed of as children.

While you certainly don't need to be in the veterinary profession to hopefully get something lasting and life-changing out of this book, I am writing based on my personal experiences working at numerous practices in five different states. I have been the sole licensed tech at many clinics, and I have been one of several at a nine-doctor practice. I have worked with dogs, cats, ferrets, reptiles, birds, cattle, horses, llamas, and many other critters over the years, but my main focus has been as a companion animal technician. I have witnessed a lot of highs and lows over the decades. I have met many amazing coworkers, clients, and patients. Several have become lifelong friends and pet sitting clients. I have hundreds of heartwarming memories, from holding newborn puppies to racing across Colorado fields on horseback rounding up Hereford bulls. But I have also been bullied more at work by adults than I ever was as a child at school. I have endured some very difficult bosses and managers—a few have been downright abusive. I have felt great anxiety and depression. I've been exhausted by the effort to be someone other than my true self. I have noticed a significant increase in the last few years of people who no longer respect other humans or animals. I have questioned why the hell I ever chose this thankless career and prayed for a way out. But out of the depths of my deepest despair, I found light, hope, and a new resolve to help others. I found stillness amid the chaos. While I don't claim to have all the answers, I know I have something to contribute to this profession, and I know I have made the lives of thousands of animals better on some level through my unique gifts. Whether it is through client education, my skills as a technician, my compassion, or my love of healing energy and integrative medicine, I try to make a positive difference daily. We all need to remember WHY we became animal caregivers in the first place. We need to find a way to reignite our passion and then share that light with our colleagues and patients. We all have enough external stressors—we don't need to be adding to our burden from inside the industry. Be the one who starts to change the culture in your corner of the world. Sometimes just a glimmer of hope may be all that is needed to save a life. It is my sincere hope that you will realize you are not alone, you are enough, and you matter. I want you to go from surviving in this industry to thriving. Be present for the animals in your care. There is a Lakota saying about being *a good relative* to all living beings, as we are all connected. The animals need you as their advocate, so be a good relative to them.

## CHAPTER 1 TAKEAWAYS

1. How has your clinic coped with the pandemic? Were there some changes that will remain permanent, such as offering curbside service?

2. What are your feelings on licensed veterinary technicians being called Veterinary Nurses?

3. Have you experienced a mental health crisis or extreme stress due to your job? Could you have handled it better?

## RESOURCES

* www.nursingworld.org
* www.navta.net
* www.avma.org (accreditation)

# CHAPTER 2: WHY WE CHOSE THIS CAREER

For many reasons, stress and burnout have become all-too-familiar side effects of the veterinary profession. We all entered college with such joy and hope for the future. You must remember *why* you got into veterinary medicine in the first place. This is your solid foundation and your base of passion to build upon. Here are the stories of my professional and personal "whys"—the reasons I chose this career and the reasons I feel I have too often been abused by it. I highly recommend the book *Find Your Why* by Simon Sinek.

## My Professional "Why"

I grew up in the quaint New England town of Sandy Hook, Connecticut. Times were different back then, and my childhood memories are happy ones. Although a dog didn't fit into our busy lifestyle, we always had cats, hamsters, and guinea pigs during my childhood, and I've loved animals as far back as I can remember. While my brother was busy playing soccer, I immersed myself in everything horse-related. If I wasn't riding them, I was reading about them, poring over magazines, or drawing blueprints for my future barn. I was considered a shy, introverted kid, but for some reason I felt confident astride an 1100-pound animal, flying over fences and galloping down wooded trails. My neighbor had two horses and a pony, and we spent hours riding through the woods and fields near our houses. I took my share of falls, but somehow I always found the courage to get back on and keep going, a lesson that has served me well. During riding lessons, my dad always told me to give him a thumbs-up when I landed on the ground, so he would know I was okay. I'm sure that watching me ride wasn't always easy on my parents—it's not the safest of sports. Although we couldn't afford a horse of my own early on, they always supported my obsession with these magical and majestic creatures, a passion that has never wavered.

It wasn't until I was in high school that I could finally start to save up for my own horse. I had a job after school and on weekends at a nearby veterinary hospital, and I cleaned stalls at a huge show barn where I took riding lessons. I fell in love with a black Quarter Horse gelding that had recently come to the barn. His registered name was Shed's Black Billy, and he was afraid of men. I started taking lessons with him and soon convinced my parents that I could save enough money to buy and board him. He was beautiful, with a coal-black coat and white star on his forehead. I was over the moon to realize my dream of owning one of these amazing creatures. I worked hard cleaning stalls, as well as feeding and turning out to pasture the dozens of horses that resided in that huge facility. On the morning of August 27,1986, I vividly remember my dad waking me up to tell me that the barn had burned to the ground. He asked if I wanted to go see if we could help. I remember being numb and probably in a state of shock as my family took the longest drive of my life. By the time we arrived at the horrific scene, there was nothing left of the eighty-four-stall barn except the charred white fencing surrounding it. I think my knees hit the ground. This was a nightmare. It was gruesome; horses were bloated and burned beyond recognition. People were sobbing at the loss of life—eighteen horses perished that night. My beautiful Billy was one of them, the only one in his section of stalls that didn't escape. I truly believe it was his fear of men that prevented him from making it to safety. Twenty people and several horses were injured, some with bad burns. A few had been hit by cars on the nearby highway as they attempted to gallop to safety. There was only one equine veterinarian at the scene, and he was beyond overwhelmed. I wish I could forget some of the images in my head from that day, but at the same time, this is why I became a veterinary technician. I had never felt so helpless. I was young, inexperienced, and emotional. There was nothing much I could do but cry and grieve with my barn friends. Days later, the cause of the fire was determined to be arson. It had been set by one of the night stablehands, who wanted to then save the horses and be a hero. When I visited the mass grave, I made a vow to Billy and the others that I have kept to this day: I would do whatever I could to care for as many animals as possible, and they would never be forgotten. *My path became clear.* I enrolled in school for Veterinary Science Technologies and later went on to Colorado State University for a degree in Equine Science. While my career path ultimately landed in small-animal medicine, I know Billy would be proud. It would be another seven years before I finally had a horse of my very own. His name is Harley, and he is my once-in-a-lifetime horse—thirty years later we are still together. His funny personality and big heart have always been a healing balm. He has been my rock throughout my entire career, sharing in all my joys and sorrows.

## My Personal "Why"

The overall feeling of helplessness and lack of control during many situations is part of what shaped my personality and made me a target for the bullying that has plagued much of my career. It's how I finally understood myself, the possible reasons *why* I was being picked on, and *why* I had certain feelings and reactions. So many things contribute to how each of us shows up in the world: genetics, culture, environment, education, and family dynamics, to name a few. My interest in self-discovery helped me acquire that understanding. It is important to note that I was unconsciously allowing my outer experiences to dictate my feelings of self-worth. Better late than never, I learned that it is your choices about your *inner* experiences that make you joyful and allow you to shine through to the outside world. *"Your personality creates your personal reality"* (Dr. Joe Dispenza).

As a child I was always called "shy," and so I believed this to be true for most of my life. Anxiety wasn't well understood or often discussed during the '70s and '80s. My teachers would comment on how quiet I was. My camp counselors would call my parents to come pick me up because I was crying again. (Honestly, I just wanted to be left alone to read a book and not be put on display during competitions and plays, which still hasn't changed.) The first noticeable crack in my foundation came in the third grade. I usually sat in the back of classrooms, so I wouldn't be noticed. One particular day, my math teacher singled me out to come to the front of the classroom and work out a problem on the blackboard. Standing up there and facing my classmates, I froze. I was petrified and subsequently humiliated at not having any answer, much less a correct one. That one moment changed me from a shy kid to a socially anxious one, although no one understood that at the time, including me. It had lasting effects, and I despise math to this day. From then on, I thought everyone was making fun of me behind my back and secretly laughing at how stupid I was. This continued for many years. In high school I didn't want to walk in front of the crowds eating lunch to stand in line for food, so I would sit at a back table and go hungry. The teenage years are hard enough on everyone without the added stress of feeling shunned. A boy I liked, who lived nearby, would visit my house after school to hang out. At school, however, he would act like he didn't know me. He would walk right past me in the hallway and stare straight ahead. His friends didn't even know about me. I was confused and hurt, and I felt like I wasn't good enough to be publicly acknowledged.

In both high school and college, I would experience shortness of breath and heart palpitations at the thought of walking in front of crowds, such as at the grandstands at football or basketball games. In college I was petrified at the thought of walking across a crowded bar to use the restroom. It didn't help my feelings of worthlessness when I was informed that my first college boyfriend had cheated on me multiple times. I don't know if this was testosterone-induced exaggeration or cold, hard truth, but I do know that I was dumbfounded and destroyed. He had claimed to love me—I had believed him. One time he threw a cinder block at me out of his second-story window because I walked out of the dormitory at the same time as another guy. He accused me of wanting to take this stranger back to my room. I was shocked—that was not part of my character at all—surely he knew that? What I didn't know at the time was that it was in *his* character to do the very thing he was accusing me of. I remember another time, standing on his dormitory stairwell after an argument, being absolutely frozen in place because although my brain told me to go back to my room, my heart wanted to go back to his. (It wasn't until many years later that I learned about the freeze response.) The worst incident, which prompted me to end our relationship, was when I took a punch to the face and blacked out. When I came to, only his roommate was there to help me. My boyfriend had hit me because I had taken his class ring off my necklace and put it on his dresser. That one small, harmless act could incite such anger was inconceivable to me.

I didn't understand it at the time, but he was my first introduction to *gaslighting* and *love bombing*: showering me with poems and letters, while telling me I was crazy when I became suspicious of anything he was doing. Accusing me of cheating when he was the one doing it, and humiliating me on a small campus, where I was sure everyone knew what he was up to except me. I don't think I was particularly naive. Like most narcissists, he was charming, as well as a really good liar and manipulator. My brain didn't have the capacity to dream up the things he was doing behind my back. That was my first and last bout with domestic violence in the physical sense, but it certainly wasn't the last instance of emotional and mental abuse that left me feeling inadequate.

My self-esteem had taken several punches to the gut over the years, but I had faith that my gut instinct was always right. *Always.* I could detect deceit from a mile away—I just *knew* when someone was lying to me. I dated some guys who gave me reverse compliments, such as "You're so ugly—I'm just kidding! Geez, you take everything so personally!" or "You're fat—just joking!" I've been told I looked like a whale in a beach photo (I was 120 pounds). I've been called by ex-girlfriends' names during intimate moments. I've had guys correct practically everything I said or did, as if I were an idiot. Their beliefs seemed to be superimposed over my own, so I always felt diminished and insignificant. I didn't know at the time that manipulators look for people with empathy to exploit in order to feed their egos, and that it had nothing to do with who I was, other than the fact that I had empathy in spades. One boyfriend used to introduce me to his friends as a veterinarian, and when I corrected him he would get mad, like my being a veterinary *technician* was embarrassing. I had another friend do the same, and when I told him I was proud of my chosen career he said, "Don't sell yourself short." Over the years I've been asked by many clients when I was going to school to become a doctor, as if being an animal nurse wasn't a profession in its own right. I believe this is partly due to a failure within our industry to adequately educate the public on the scope of our education, knowledge, and skill.

I wish I'd had more self-esteem over the years to get out of some of these relationships sooner and stand up for myself with more authority, instead of giving years of my life to the wrong partner. The manner in which I was treated helped mold the insecure person I became, which made me more vulnerable to all manner of mistreatment, personally and professionally.

I've had many wonderful relationships as well, and I hold those dear to my heart. My very first boyfriend is someone I can always count on as our close friendship has spanned decades. As I became older and wiser, I no longer had any tolerance for mind games, lying, or cheating. I had no patience for someone who pretended to love my animals but truthfully barely liked them, and on one occasion asked me to get rid of them. Instead, I got rid of *him*. When that special person finally comes along who treats me as nothing less than an equal partner, I'm all in. Until then, life is good with minimal drama. Which is why I don't need to deal with it at work, and neither do you. We need to become peaceful islands in an ocean of chaos, so others may reach our shores to feel safe and included.

*"Those who find a 'why' to live, can bear almost any 'how'."* (Viktor Frankl)

## CHAPTER 2 TAKEAWAYS

1. What is your professional "why"?

2. What is your personal "why" that helps to define your personality? Can you find a way to serve the person you once were and make a difference in someone's life?

3. Have you experienced anxiety? What does it feel like?

## RESOURCES

* *Find Your Why* by Simon Sinek
* *Best Self: Be You, Only Better* by Mike Bayer
* *Loving What Is* by Byron Katie
* www.joyfuldvm.com

# PART ONE: TOXIC PEOPLE

*"I'm not who I think I am. I'm not who you think I am. I'm who I think you think I am."*

The above quote rang so true for me. I forget who said it, but I liked the saying so much, I wrote it down in a notebook. For those of us who are stuck in caring too much about what other people think, which is what toxic people thrive on, this will ring true for you as well.

## CHAPTER 3: ANXIETY AND HIGH SENSITIVITY

If only my parents or teachers had known about *anxiety* while I was growing up, maybe I could have had some better tools to cope. No one is to blame—it just wasn't a fixture in our terminology like it is today. That word didn't show up in my life with any meaning until I was well into my 40s, and a coworker was discussing her struggles with it. Suddenly a light bulb went on, and I thought, *That's me!* While I mostly have situational anxiety when feeling judged or overwhelmed, many suffer from a chronic condition known as generalized anxiety disorder. The same symptoms show up: heart palpitations, sweating, worrying, restless mind, shortness of breath, and difficulty sleeping. You're caught in this seemingly endless loop. The old adage holds that in the past, humans had anxiety because they needed the adrenaline to keep them on their toes to avoid being attacked by a tiger lurking nearby. Remind yourself that *there is no tiger.* When I learned this, many things finally started to make sense. I no longer labeled myself as shy, because I make friends easily and enjoy interacting with clients. I go on vacations by myself and meet lifelong friends. I am an introvert, but this just means I need to be alone to recharge my batteries. I've never had much of a fight-or-flight response, like you always hear about when dealing with adrenaline and fear. I freeze instead. I first learned that this was another coping response at a conference where the speaker was talking about animals, especially cats, freezing when scared. They make themselves as small, still, and unnoticeable as possible. Again, I thought, *That's me!* (No wonder I understand cats so well!) I thought back to that time in elementary math class, and in college when I was literally frozen on the dorm steps, unable to make a decision or move any part of my body. I started researching anxiety, so I could understand myself and my reactions better. Looking back over my life, I saw so many situations where anxiety had overtaken me. During those times, I had no idea what was "wrong" with me.

Anxiety sometimes got the best of me throughout my childhood and college years when I was showing horses. I would go over and over the jumping course in my mind, even if it was just four jumps in a circle twice around. Once I got in the ring in front of spectators, my mind would go blank, and I wouldn't breathe. On the long drives through the New York countryside on the way to college horse shows, I would get dizzy if I closed my eyes, and my knuckles would be white from gripping the van seat in front of me. I would be so nauseated that I couldn't eat when we stopped for breakfast. On more than one occasion, when we got to the barn I told my coach that I wasn't riding in my class. It was debilitating and embarrassing, but I couldn't help the way my body reacted. I had no words to adequately describe my feelings, nor any coping skills, and my teammates were probably exasperated with me. When I did win a ribbon, it was always a shock to me.

I'll never forget one time when I got a major boost of unexpected confidence. I was a member of the Horse Judging Team at Colorado State (I took this class in lieu of Public Speaking). We had the privilege of traveling to some amazing horse farms in Texas and Oklahoma. I met world-famous Quarter Horses on that trip, the purpose of which was to prepare us for a future competition with several other colleges. For hours we did round after round of judging, four horses in each round. We had to place them in the correct order of body conformation or performance and stand alone in front of a judge, projecting our voice as we went over every aspect of horseflesh from memory. When the competition was over, our teacher announced the individual results. Among dozens of competitors, "Tracy, you came in third." I'm pretty sure I looked behind me to see who this other Tracy was. My teacher laughed and pointed at me, "Yes, you!" I had never been so proud of an achievement! I had behaved my way to success. For once I didn't freeze, and this was before I knew about any of the tools I'm going to share with you. This defining moment gave me a taste of the confidence I needed to realize there was a better way to present myself.

Once I finally understood I had this condition called anxiety, I still felt that something was missing. I was constantly told I was "too sensitive" and "took everything personally." Yes, that is all true, but people were saying it as if it was *wrong* for me to have those feelings. I couldn't change who I was any more than I could change the color of my eyes. I felt undermined, and all the messages I was receiving led to constant feelings of inadequacy. Every time I spoke my truth, I was shut down and brushed off. People always wanted *me* to change, yet if I mentioned someone else's comments or actions, I was typically told, "That's just the way they are." It reminds me of a time that I was pulled over for speeding. I mentioned to the cop that I was just trying to keep up with traffic and that many others were passing me and he said "Yeah, well, I pulled *you* over." Even now, others' verbal abuse is almost always excused or justified, as if my own feelings have no merit. I really don't care if Nancy is having a bad day because her child is sick; that does not give her the right to launch a verbal attack on anyone else. While you can't change other people, only your reactions to them, this doesn't mean you should accept abuse in any form. I wish these people would practice the Five-Minute Rule: set a timer for five minutes and go somewhere to rant, rave, cry, complain, etc. Once you get all your feelings out in the allotted time, you follow it with the Five-Second Rule, saying "5, 4, 3, 2, 1, Go!" and making the conscious choice to be a nicer person toward any innocent bystanders. *The 5 Second Rule* by Mel Robbins explains in detail how this can be used for anything you're on the fence about. It's a version of "Just do it." I use it to get out of bed some mornings!

At long last, the missing puzzle piece I was seeking showed up in the form of a book called *The Highly Sensitive Person* by Elaine Aron. I FINALLY felt understood, by myself if no one else. I was in my late 40s at this point—better late than never! Being highly sensitive is a genetic trait, not a personality flaw—something I had intuitively felt all along. Highly sensitive people (HSPs) process stimuli more thoroughly than the general population and pick up on subtleties in the environment that others never notice. This is termed *clairsentience*, or clear feeling. This can be a detriment, as it feels as if everything around you, both positive and negative, melds with your energy field. Large crowds drain us, strong scents agitate us, loud or repetitive noises drive us insane because of our overly sensitive nervous systems (try concentrating at work with continuously barking dogs and multiple conversations going on). HSPs are conditioned to doubt themselves from an early age, which can lead to impostor syndrome, anxiety, and depression. We become sponges for the emotions of others and are often targeted by narcissistic, toxic people who need a parasitic relationship to feed their ego and desire for control (where they suck the life out of you and leave you desiccated). Boy do I know about that!

For the first time, so many things from my past made sense. I hit the ground running with my newfound information and haven't stopped researching and reading and taking courses to better understand myself and others like me. It now makes sense that I need to be alone and quiet to recharge my batteries and calm my nervous system (this is also a classic need of introverts). It makes sense that conflict and criticism can have devastating effects on an HSP's self-worth. I now see myself as a highly sensitive, empathic introvert with situational anxiety. (I don't necessarily like labels, but this is *my* definition, so I have an anchor point from which to better understand my feelings and actions.) I no longer see this as a detriment but as my suit of armor—my symbols of strength and power, so I can seek true peace. I have to remind myself that bullies and narcissists themselves aren't confident people. Obnoxious behavior is their way of blustering to cover up their deep insecurities. It's those of us who are aware of and stand tall in our truth, whatever that may be, that are the strong ones.

It's far from easy and a constant struggle at times, this feeling of being a magnet for other people's toxicity. It doesn't help that humans have what's termed negativity bias, where we're hardwired to remember the bad things over the good. It takes many "Good job!" accolades to outweigh one "You're worthless!" (whether spoken or implied). It's not easy when you think you work hard but have no constructive feedback to indicate whether you're living up to expectations. Sometimes the goalposts you're aiming for keep getting moved, so you can never win the game. Gaslighters, narcissists, and other toxic people will always seek me out to try to extinguish my torch, but at least now I can see the wolf outline under their sheep's clothing. Now I have a better understanding of *why* I get picked on and have a toolbox of coping skills to rely on. If you see parts of yourself in anything I have gone through, I hope I can shine a light for you on a path to inner peace that was once so dark for me. Together, let's create a solid foundation for a happy, fulfilling life, both personally and in our chosen profession.

## CHAPTER 3 TAKEAWAYS

1. How do you struggle to define your feelings or emotions?

2. Do you suffer from feelings of worthlessness? If so, how do you deal with them?

3. Do you have a hard time expressing your feelings and hate conflict? How do you cope in those moments?

4. Have you been gaslighted by someone you trusted? Have you known you were right, only to be told you're crazy? How did you feel in those situations?

## RESOURCES

* *Sensitive Is the New Strong* by Anita Moorjani
* *Don't You Know Who I Am?* by Ramani S. Durvasula
* *The 5 Second Rule* by Mel Robbins
* *Toxic People: The Rules of the Game* by Neil Iton
* *The Highly Sensitive Person's Guide to Dealing With Toxic People* by Shahida Arabi
* *Real Happiness* by Sharon Salzberg
* *Fierce Conversations* by Susan Scott
* *Get Out of Your Head* by Jennie Allen

# CHAPTER 4: ENERGY VAMPIRES AND BULLIES

I once heard a saying that the cracks in your personal foundation are there to let the light in. I believe these cracks start *in your mind*—the chipping away at your self-esteem by toxic individuals. No one is born thinking they aren't good enough. That happens slowly, over time. As children we are encouraged to walk and talk—we're cheered on for doing so. As we get older, we're told to sit down and shut up. We're told our ideas are stupid, and our opinions don't matter. We are invalidated at every turn, or at least it can feel that way at times. The criticism and conflict can have devastating effects on our psyches. Constantly feeling unworthy can lead to depression and suicidal ideations. Once other people's negativity stops, we tend to continue it, which perpetuates the problem. *Maybe I'm really not good enough at this. Maybe I don't deserve that. Perhaps I'm not smart enough to take that on.* These cracks in our foundation also allow our positive thoughts to leak out and become lost in the ether. Over time, the fissures get wider, and we are invalidated in multiple areas of our lives. This is not a good or sustainable space to be in. All any human ultimately wants is to be validated. Whether from our family, friends, romantic partner, or coworkers, we just want to feel welcomed. *I matter. I am heard. I am understood. I belong.*

The cracks often start out as insidious hairline fractures—offhand comments by someone who matters to you that make you begin to doubt yourself. Nothing you do is ever good enough. That nagging voice in your head starts to question your own thoughts and beliefs. Soon the unworthiness envelops and kidnaps your self-esteem. Like an abandoned building, the cracks grow wider, and the foundation crumbles. Until you understand that the light can also sneak in through those cracks and bring healing to your mindset, the negative internal dialogue will continue.

First, you need to be aware that this is even happening. *You can't change what you don't acknowledge* (thank you, Dr. Phil, for that piece of advice). You are continuing the legacy of your emotional abusers, whether in professional or personal relationships, and giving them power long after they are out of your sight. Second, you have to believe you are worthy of a better, happier life. It's not easy work, but it's worth the effort to rebuild your foundation until it is strong and solid. You can stand tall in your truth and use your newfound confidence as a shield to deflect the toxic spears of self-doubt hurled by others in your direction. Throughout this book, I will help you navigate how to do this.

Once I came to terms with the notion that I was a highly sensitive, empathic introvert with situational anxiety, I could get to work on changing my mindset about what that meant. I'm finding strength in knowing I can change my *reactions* to any given situation. It will always be a work in progress. Sometimes it feels like two steps forward and one step back, but as long as there is a forward, positive progression, I feel like I'm on the right path. Have compassion for yourself during this process. You are far from the only one going through bullying and gaslighting—I witness it constantly. Like I've said, I've been bullied and made fun of far more at work than I ever was at school.

Some of the worst things I was called as a kid were Slender Spaghetti, String Bean, and Bookworm (names I certainly wouldn't mind as a middle-aged adult). The workplace, on the other hand, can be brutal. I will probably never understand why toxic individuals are given free license to treat others however they want, while the sympathetic, kind, compassionate ones always have to explain themselves and be on the defensive. If I mention to management how a coworker is rude or abusive, I'm told that I'm "too sensitive," and the offender is let off the hook. I've witnessed some veterinarians being meaner to their technicians than they are to assistants, which has never made much sense, as we are supposed to be their right hand on the patient care team. What you put out energetically to the universe will boomerang back to you. Our patients, who are already nervous and stressed, pick up on any negative energy the staff is experiencing. I often feel this is very unfair to them. No matter how well we try to hide our emotions, animals are barometers of truth, and it has an impact on them.

Start your day with a few simple positive affirmations: *I am enough. Love always wins. Today I will be a light in the darkness* . . . whatever rings true for you. Do this when you first wake up to set your intention for the day. A little trick I use to help with my negative thought loop is to wear a bracelet that is easy to move from one wrist to the other. Every time I catch myself thinking something judgmental about myself or others, I move the bracelet. Trust me, I get tired of moving it, but the point is to bring awareness to my thoughts. You can't change what you don't notice or acknowledge. Another trick I use is to carry a small stone or crystal in my pocket. Every time I remember it's there,

I think of something I'm grateful for. I also believe in their individual energetic properties and choose one that feels right for that day. At one particular job, which you will read about next, I was carrying a black stone called Jet in my pocket, which is said to absorb negative energy. In the middle of a surgery, I felt it crack, then break into several pieces in my pocket. As I had never experienced anything like this before, I took the pieces to two different rock and crystal shops and was told the same thing by both: that the stone had taken an energetic bullet for me. Somehow, I wasn't surprised. I was advised to bury it, so any negative remnants could be absorbed by the earth.

If you are truly depressed or overly anxious and having a lot of negative or dark thoughts, please seek out a qualified doctor or therapist—there is no shame in getting help. There are definitely times when prescription medication may be warranted, and I'll be the first to admit that no matter how many holistic tools I have access to, there have been times when they weren't enough. When you're so beaten down by others that you can't see the light, medication may be just enough to stop or slow down the cascade of thoughts wreaking havoc on your mind and body. Just be sure the doctor listens to your concerns and gives you a correct diagnosis. I have been picked on and bullied at multiple jobs, and sometimes it feels like death by a thousand cuts. I've been completely ignored by the boss who greeted everyone else and had my paychecks tossed in my general direction instead of handed to me. I've politely mentioned that an occasional "thank-you" would be appreciated, only to be told, "I sign your paycheck. That's your thank-you." I've been told I was disposable the day after my best friend was fired for speaking up at a staff meeting. I had one manager tell me, a week after I started, that because I made "so much," she couldn't give "her girls" (the receptionists) raises. Not only was I made to feel like I wasn't worth my paycheck, but all my education and experience were dismissed. There is pervasive favoritism everywhere. I've had bruises on my arms from being grabbed by a manager who didn't think I'd cleaned the windows to her satisfaction. Chairs have been kicked out from under me when I just wanted to sit down for a few minutes. I have asked for a raise after thirteen years without one, only to be told I didn't deserve one, because the manager looked up the average salary for licensed vet technicians, and I already exceeded that amount. What's *average* about thirty years in the business, two college degrees, and multiple certifications in various areas of animal care? Let me be clear: unlike RNs, licensed techs typically make less than $20/hour for their entire career, unless they work in emergency or specialty medicine. I personally haven't ever been given a cost-of-living increase. Why is this injustice allowed to persist?

Nothing thus far had compared to the abuse I was to experience at what I will call Toxic Swamp Vet Clinic (TSVC), a place that was beautiful on the outside but hid a suppressive culture, led by the manager and enforced by the owner. This was where I finally hit rock bottom. I no longer had the will to keep going. I couldn't understand why I was constantly singled out and treated like I was worthless. Why couldn't my boss and manager appreciate that I was smart, kind, hardworking, and reliable? I knew my worth but felt that others didn't, which resulted in constant fear for my financial security. It's harder to leave a job than a personal relationship in some instances, because you can't always speak your mind without the fear of being fired. We're supposed to put up and shut up. I had constant negative thoughts going through my mind. I knew I didn't deserve to be physically sick before work every day or to go home at lunch and cry for an hour. My eyelid would twitch for days, and I would break out in hives. I couldn't find relief from the constant mental and emotional abuse. Self-doubt began to infiltrate my mind in all areas: *I must be dumb, my skill set sucks, the animals deserve a better nurse, what am I doing in this profession, anyway?* I wanted out. Yet at the same time, I felt stuck. The vet industry was all I knew, and I wasn't getting any younger. I saw no solution, and I felt an overwhelming sense of despair and depression. I also knew that no matter how dark my thoughts became, I wouldn't do anything to endanger myself. While I could maybe explain my decision to my family and friends, so they would have some sort of closure, I couldn't explain to my animals why I would leave them behind. Looking into their soulful eyes full of unconditional love was enough reason to keep going. We depended on each other.

One particular day, my Toxic Swamp boss sought me out after lunch. He looked me in the eyes and said, "Last Wednesday when we worked together, I thought the day went very smoothly. You did a really good job, and we worked well together." I felt such a rush of gratitude at finally being noticed and validated, until he lightly smacked my arm and said with amusement, "Tracy, I wasn't even here that day! Remember, it was my golf tournament!" He chuckled and walked away, leaving me standing there, frozen in shock and disbelief. *Who says that?* I could feel the tears welling up and threatening to overspill my eyelids. I will never forget that humiliating moment as long as I live. Any ounce of confidence I had left plummeted to the ground. Even one of the relief vets relentlessly picked on me and put me in my place, saying things like, "If I want your opinion, I'll ask for it" when I was simply speaking up as an experienced vet tech. He also told me in no uncertain terms to "Stop bothering the clients about nutrition," when I was just doing my job of educating clients about proper care of their pets, something I am passionate about. This person had known me and treated me respectfully for years—I can only assume he got wrapped up in the toxicity and pack mentality. It was such a shame, because everyone there practiced high-quality medicine, and the clinic had a good reputation in the community. One bad apple with too much power can indeed ruin the entire basket.

Another memorable moment at TSVC was when I was told that I was being considered for the leader of the technical staff. The manager called me on my day off and told me I really needed to be at the meeting that night. I informed her that I had just undergone a breast biopsy and wasn't feeling well (not to mention the mental stress of worrying about the results). She told me I "wouldn't be disappointed," and she really wanted me there. This particular meeting was a big deal, complete with a full meal cooked by the boss. All of the staff would be attending, so I pulled myself together and went. Partway through the meal, the manager made the announcement that one of the newer assistants, I'll call her Laura, got the leadership job. She would now have power over me, a licensed veterinary technician of over twenty years. I could feel so many pairs of eyes on me. I don't know if it was shock and disbelief or pity, but I could barely choke down my food or meet their eyes. Once dessert was served, I took the high road and went over to congratulate Laura. The next day at work, she told me that I was the only person to do so, and she really appreciated it. To this day I wonder why the manager told me I "wouldn't be disappointed" if I attended the meeting. I believe it was just her nasty streak reveling in my humiliation. The saying is true that employees typically leave managers, not practices.

I felt constantly judged and demeaned in that corrupt environment, and I ultimately ended up in the hospital emergency room due to overwhelming stress. My heart rate was through the roof, I couldn't stand up straight, and I couldn't stop vomiting. I was now falling apart physically as well as mentally and emotionally. I had so many triggers that would cause anxiety attacks—it took years to regain my previous technical skill level. My boss was constantly on my case if I couldn't hit a vein on the first try, every single time. One of the assistants was always running to him to tattle on me, and he'd come marching over to proclaim, "You can't feel that? You can't find that?" and grab the syringe out of my hand. We were all constantly monitored on camera by the manager, sitting in her locked office. I couldn't take a deep breath, my heart would pound, and my hands would shake with anxiety. I became incapable of drawing blood or placing catheters—it's amazing how inept you can become with someone constantly judging you and telling you how awful you are. Thank God I eventually got those skills back, because my superpower is putting catheters in angry, ancient, dehydrated cats. Several well-meaning coworkers who knew of my issue would try to encourage me by saying,

"Just pretend it's a cat" when I was trying to get blood from a large dog. I still have situations that trigger my anxiety, residual effects that may never go away. If you find yourself in a stressful, judgmental, and demeaning environment in any situation, professional or personal, get out sooner rather than later. Your health and sanity depend on it!

One thing that helped me cling to sanity during this time was my love of energy healing, particularly a modality known as Reiki (pronounced ray-key). Reiki, the Japanese term for universal life-force energy, is a method of relaxation that allows the body to begin the healing process (see Chapter 13). Unfortunately, I wasn't allowed to even mention Reiki at Toxic Swamp, as my very religious yet hypocritical boss looked it up online and saw that it had "Buddhist roots." He told me that he almost didn't hire me because of it (I had mentioned it on my resume because I was proud of my complementary holistic skills). I explained that it was nonreligious and practiced by people from all faiths around the world, but there was no convincing him it wasn't some type of witchcraft.

Soon after my hospital visit, I had an upcoming energy healing class on the spiritual/angelic realm, but I almost canceled because I was still so depressed and stuck that I didn't feel like doing anything. This class was being taught by one of the foremost Reiki Master Teachers in the world, and it wasn't often he came to the United States, let alone to Virginia. I knew it was the chance of a lifetime. Plus, many of my energy healing friends would be there. Surely I could count on their positive vibes to help me get back to my normal, laughing self. Boy was I mistaken. Instead, I felt like my friends ganged up on me to tell me to stop being so negative, and that others had it much worse. I was told I should act more like another friend, who had a bubbly, outgoing personality. I knew that many others had problems far worse than mine, but that shouldn't devalue my own pain. I could barely breathe. I couldn't form words. I was devastated, and yet again, invalidated. I wanted someone to *listen* to me, not berate me. Somehow I found the strength to make it to class the next day, and luckily the familiar, peaceful setting of the Reiki Center and the quiet wisdom of my longtime teacher had a calming effect on me. That soothed the rough edges of my soul, so I was able to be fully present for the three-day class.

At one point, our teacher from Germany stopped talking mid-sentence and miraculously said that his spiritual guides (such as guardian angels) were in communication with ours, and if a message came across that seemed to be specifically for one of us, it was. The example he used was thinking about suicide. I don't want to think that I was at that point, but I definitely wanted a way out of my current dire situation and all the mental anguish I was experiencing. I sat there in stunned silence. He said to listen to your heart, not the fear. Do what makes your soul happy. Being spiritually realized is to accept things as they are (more on this later), and if others are cruel, it is a misuse of their free will. He mentioned trauma and PTSD and that *the world isn't made better by people who stay stuck in a daily routine that isn't feeding their soul.* I was mesmerized. It was as if a huge weight had been lifted off me, and I felt a warm glow of hope. A higher frequency of energy buzzed around me as I soaked up his wisdom. I truly believe that class and those words saved me, showing me that clawing myself out of the muck would be worth it one day. If you're reading this book, know that it was.

After class, I went back to my hotel room and brainstormed with my roommate about ways to escape my current job situation. As I was also a professional pet sitter, I focused on that as a way to earn a living wage and still do work I loved. Those clients always praised me and treated me with respect and trust. I drove home at the end of the weekend energized, with a renewed sense of hope and purpose.

Unfortunately, that feeling was short-lived. I arrived home from the class late at night, exhausted but excited to share my adventure with my parents, who were pet sitting for me while I was away. As soon as I entered my house, a heavy energy cloaked me. My first thought was that something was wrong with one of my parents or animals, but a quick look at Mom's face told me silently that Dad was in one of his moods. The wind went right out of my sails. I had been away for three days. What could I possibly have done to upset him? I remember him stepping over my suitcase in the hallway and going to bed for the night without saying a word to me. I'm sure Mom tried to smooth things over, but I was distraught. As often happened when I was made to feel less than, it felt like all my energy drained out the bottoms of my feet into the earth. Needless to say, I didn't sleep much that night.

The next morning I crept downstairs for coffee, time I normally enjoyed spending with Mom. But Dad was waiting for me at the kitchen table, and a two-hour rant ensued, which culminated in him telling me I didn't have the discipline to run my own pet sitting business, and I needed to stay at my current job because it paid the bills and covered my health insurance. Besides, I had a lot of animals that needed me and a house to care for. Yes, it was the financially safe option, but I could sense the depression creeping back in. My wings had essentially been clipped, and I felt demeaned for having my own thoughts and feelings, for needing to be true to myself. So I stayed at that job, and my soul suffered some more. I had to find ways to better understand and navigate people's motives.

## CHAPTER 4 TAKEAWAYS

1. Who or what are the energy vampires in your life?

2. Whose toxic rhetoric do you keep repeating in your head, long after they've left?

3. Do you have an escape plan to leave your current situation if it isn't nourishing your soul?

4. What positive affirmations can you repeat to yourself to combat the negativity fed to you by others?

5. Do you have a habit (like moving a bracelet) to help you remember to keep your inner thoughts positive?

## RESOURCES

* National Suicide Prevention Hotline (800) 273-8255 or 988 (new in 2021)
* www.veterinarysuicideawareness.com
* www.nomv.org (Not One More Vet)
* AVMA cyber bullying hotline (626) 531-1140
* www.stopbullying.gov

* *The Warrior Goddess Training Program* by HeatherAsh Amara
* *Psychic Shield* by Caitlin Matthews
* *The Four Agreements* by Don Miguel Ruiz

# CHAPTER 5: GASLIGHTERS AND NARCISSISTS

I had no one to share my thoughts with at home, so I had to work everything out on my own. My main way of escaping reality has always been to read, and I read dozens of self-discovery books, trying to figure out what was wrong with *me*, as I was the common denominator in all of this. While I could count on my friends and family to listen and offer advice under certain circumstances, it was hard to explain the extent of what I was going through, and I didn't want to become a burden to anyone. Sometimes you just need someone to hold space for you while you vent or talk things out—to listen and honor your reality.

Because I use the following terms in this book, I will define them here. They can be traits of coworkers or more personal relationships. Either way, be aware of what you're dealing with. I'm not a psychologist, but I've done a lot of research, and these definitions reflect my understanding of these unfavorable traits. The word *gaslighting* originated with a 1938 play by Patrick Hamilton, in which the husband would dim the gas lights in the house and tell his wife she was crazy when she noticed. A gaslighter erodes and invalidates your reality until you rely on them for the perceived truth they feed you. They make you feel like you blow everything out of proportion and take things too personally, despite all evidence to the contrary. This insidious form of manipulation can be very disorienting as you try to separate reality from deceit. Gaslighting can be part of a *narcissistic personality disorder,* which is characterized by a sense of entitlement, feelings of superiority, and a great need for admiration. Such people have feelings of grandiosity and often behave childishly if they don't get their way, even throwing tantrums. Although narcissists can have deep emotions, they lack empathy for others. You may not understand why they cry watching *The Notebook* but remain unemotional when you tell them a dear friend is in the hospital. Narcissists are typically very charming and can have many admirers, most of whom they exploit for their own gain, whether that's money, sex, praise, or attention. These types seek out people who are sensitive and emotionally responsive, such as healers and rescuers, and they use that against them to feed their narcissism. Unfortunately, this can lead to a *trauma bond* with an abuser, draining you physically and emotionally until you feel isolated and worthless in a kind of learned helplessness. This trauma gets trapped in our bodies and can lead to all manner of mental and physical ailments.

*Love bombing* occurs when an abuser feeds into your need to be cherished and validated. They flatter and charm you, but they can typically only keep this up for about six months, at the most. It's the honeymoon phase before their true colors appear. This is why they typically move fast to establish an intimate relationship, so they can devalue and control you. Once you're on to their character and attempt to leave, they often try *hoovering*, and like the vacuum cleaner attempt to suck you back in. Be aware that they don't actually miss you—they miss *controlling* you. If hoovering doesn't work, you may become the victim of a smear campaign. Make no mistake—these charming manipulators have a circus of trained monkeys to back them up and assist with your character assassination.

*Breadcrumbing* is similar to love bombing. The toxic person makes you think they have changed and that they truly love you. They leave little "breadcrumbs," such as texting that they miss you, coming home for dinner on time for a week straight, surprising you with flowers . . . but please don't set your bar for happiness so low that these little gestures mean anything more than a way to weave you deeper into their web. Narcissists often revert to what's termed *word salad*, which is when they deflect, blame, and bring up conflicts from long ago to confuse you and throw you off track. This is never relevant to the current situation you are trying to discuss. You may walk away scratching your head, wondering why his failure to return home last night is somehow your fault. You may know intellectually that you are not the crazy one and that you deserve better, yet still be unable to escape the abuse cycle—you keep following those breadcrumbs and melt every time you get love bombed with promises for a better future. This could be due to biochemical reactions that create an intense bond between a victim and an abuser. The unpredictability of hot and cold treatment creates an endless loop of excitement and fear, leading to feelings of infatuation and addiction. There are many hormones involved in this that affect the brain. I was once caught in a relationship like this, and even though I knew intellectually that it wasn't a good situation, I couldn't seem to get out. At the time I was unaware of the addiction/infatuation cycle, but it now makes sense. Make no mistake: there is no love involved here. The constant hypercriticism, making you feel unworthy and deficient, can really affect all aspects of your life. You need to leave these toxic people in your rearview mirror, and don't let them see any brake lights!

While a narcissist's behavioral traits are usually hardwired from childhood due to being spoiled and entitled, there are also your garden-variety toxic people, who usually don't realize the impact they are having on those around them. They may ask how your day was, then interrupt you mid-sentence to talk about themselves or turn to talk to someone else. Do you have coworkers like this? They may overstep boundaries, invade your personal space, exhibit attention-seeking behavior, and suck you dry emotionally. However, if you point this out to them, they may be willing to improve their behavior. I call this the difference between your Average Joe and Cottonmouth Joe. (Every time I dream about snakes, it's a warning to protect or inform me. One time I dreamed about a puppy that turned into a cobra, and I woke up knowing exactly who I had to beware of. Another time it was an anaconda who lived under the vet clinic, and that human snake turned out to be one of the worst managers ever. Never underestimate the power of your intuition.)

It was imperative that I found ways to cope at this job I felt stuck in. I called on my spiritual helpers, my angels and spirit guides. I prayed. I looked for Plans B and C while living Plan A. I tried my best to be *mindful* of my thoughts and feelings, and not to just robotically plow ahead. At TSVC, I enjoyed the large majority of my coworkers—we could sympathize because we were all on the same sinking ship. However, commiserating with your teammates keeps all of you stuck in the mire of a negativity loop. After two years, many jumped ship or were forced to walk the plank, like I was. There were thirty-three of us who had quit or were fired by the time I was handed my box of belongings and escorted to my car by Laura, the head vet assistant, of all people. My boss called the mass exodus "God weeding the garden." It was baffling to all of us, because he wouldn't even listen to his longtime employees about the manipulative, backstabbing behavior of the current manager. I was called into the office and told that no one liked working with me. (Strange, as I'm still good friends with many of them, and they all swear they would never have said that, especially to that manager.) I was told that I was "stealing everyone's happiness." (No, your manager and the culture she perpetuates is.) I also found it interesting that the next technician to be fired was given almost exactly the same speech. I'm convinced that Golden Retrievers have a manual they all read at birth about how to carry a leash in their mouths, and pugs have one with instructions on how to make nail trims as difficult as possible ("If all else fails, turn blue"). I'm also convinced there's a secret manager's manual titled *Team Building 101: How to Tear People to Shreds and Expect Them to Do Better,* by Managers without a Clue.

I actually felt a huge sense of relief as I drove away, even though I didn't know what I was going to do next. I tried to find humor in the humiliation—I had been barely treading water there for two years due to the poisonous culture, and *I* was the one to blame for people's unhappiness? I was also the one who had been told several times by the boss to be quiet because I laugh too much. So was I too happy or too unhappy? Anything I attempted to say to voice *my* point of view was brushed off as nonsense or quashed from the start. Several of us have ended up at other jobs together and still get along just fine. Pet parents want consistency in their pet's care team. I know there were many inquiries from owners about what was going on behind the scenes.

Training new staff is expensive and time-consuming. It's so much more efficient to value and train the staff you already have. Take the time to give and receive feedback on a regular basis before the train derails. It's usually the quiet, unassuming staff members who know what's truly going on behind the scenes. If you've ever seen footage of a wild horse herd, the lead mare isn't necessarily the strongest or most outgoing, but the most *aware.* She is the one who will ultimately warn the herd of danger. Leadership is an ongoing practice of awareness, not just a title.

A few years later, I had a manager at yet another clinic who also must have read "the manual." I worked hard every day. I gave my best. I was often the first one at work. I was reliable, responsible, compassionate, trustworthy, and a team player. I enjoyed going to this job every day and working alongside my teammates—I saw them as my extended family. We laughed and joked and worked well together caring for our patients. Therefore, I was completely blindsided when the manager called me into the office one day and promptly said, "You're not going to like this," followed by a two-hour attack on me, personally and professionally. It was like I had been floating peacefully on a calm ocean before a shark breached, intent on devouring me. Everything positive I believed about myself was blasted out of the water. I was told I was unorganized, I couldn't multitask, I didn't know how to prioritize, I had a "black cloud over my head," and no one liked working with me. I swear that's in Chapter One of their manual! (By the way, it's been scientifically proven that when people stop multitasking and focus on one thing at a time, productivity increases by 40%.) I was accused of being "too linear," whatever that means. To me it sounded like being organized and methodical, like having all my ducks in a row, something I would think would be appreciated in a surgical tech. When I asked what was wrong with being linear, I was told, "The world doesn't work that way." By now I was completely confused, and when I attempted to speak up I was told, "Your perception isn't reality" and "No one wants to tell you the truth." Talk about gaslighting! And the best yet, I was told I needed to see a therapist! *For what?* I wondered. Words are harsh and can hurt worse than a physical punch to the gut. I was so overwhelmed by all the negativity and accusations being dumped on me that my sensitive brain shut down (which I was also accused of doing, as if I could help it). What made it even worse was that I liked this manager and thought we had a good personal and professional relationship. This one conversation broke that bond forever, mainly because it wasn't a conversation at all, but an ambush.

I could no longer find words, and my mind was going numb trying to rapidly process all of this. I felt the fear of losing the job I loved clenching my stomach, like one of those nautical knots that people use as doorstops, tight and intricate and heavy. Sure enough, I was warned that if I wanted to keep my job, I would have to work really, really hard. I truly couldn't understand how I was going to work any harder than I already was, even though I was told, "Everyone works circles around you," which was so far from the truth it was almost laughable. I was always busy and rarely got even a few minutes of downtime. When I brought up a few others who were always on their phones or standing around holding up the counters while I ran around like a chicken with its head cut off, excuses were made for them. Favoritism at its finest. I was told that I stand around and watch my assistants do all the work, which is 100% unequivocally a lie. If anything, I've been told on numerous occasions by my assistants to stop cleaning, that I had more important things to do. I've been told that I am their reason for wanting to become a vet tech. If I'm working on a weekend, my coworkers say "Yay!" with a big smile. When I'm in the back in surgery all morning, they say "I missed you!" when I finally make it back up front. We work as a team, and I've always tried to foster those relationships. The majority of my friends are former and current coworkers spanning decades. Therefore, I couldn't believe what I was hearing. Trust me, I am very aware of my strengths and weaknesses and am my own harshest critic. I knew all these horrible accusations weren't true! Everything I was being told I was failing at, I believed was one of my strengths. It was like Opposite Day. Those allegations did not reflect my values or work ethic. Speaking of ethics, I found out that this manager called one of my coworkers and told her *every detail* of our meeting! Later I talked to most of my teammates privately, imploring them to be honest with me. Every single one swore they didn't know what on earth I was talking about, let alone that they had told the manager they didn't enjoy working with me. I was even told more than once, "You're one of my favorite people," "You're one of the kindest people I know," and "I love working with you!" Unless they are all Oscar-worthy actors, I'm pretty good at recognizing the truth when I see it. These are people I consider friends—we talk and text and hang out outside of work. Yet here I was feeling isolated, as intended, by my manager's comments. Who could I really trust? Pitting people against each other is classic. I would have gone to my bosses, but I was led to believe they knew about this meeting and were in agreement with the content. I went from having a normal day to feeling like an utter failure, fearing for my job. I honestly didn't think it could ever get worse than my TSVC experience, yet here I was, suddenly at one of the lowest points of my career.

I just kept working hard *as I always had*, but mentally I was feeling far from okay. (If I didn't need a therapist before, I sure did now.) My anxiety went into overdrive, and I once again became depressed. My self-worth was at an all-time low. I loved this job and my coworkers and clients—how could I fight to keep it when I didn't even understand *why* I was being attacked? I came close to ending up in the hospital again, as my resting heart rate was so elevated. A coworker even called the police to do a welfare check on me because she was afraid I would have a heart attack. Interestingly, I was soon told by this same manager what a fabulous job I was doing, that I was "knocking it out of the park," and that the bosses were impressed, even though I wasn't doing anything differently, which was confirmed by my equally baffled but amused coworkers. We never had a cross word after that, but the fear for my livelihood never left. Oddly, about a year later, one of the other technicians went through the same bombardment and was told very similar things. A third tech also disclosed that she had been told no one liked working with her either. I personally never heard that from any of our coworkers about any of us. I wondered who would be next on the chopping block. I don't understand why so many managers seem to be threatened by licensed technicians. We don't want their job, we just want to be able to do ours in a supportive and harmonious environment. We want an advocate who has our backs and understands the stresses of the job without piling on more. Trust me, if we wanted to manage people all day, we wouldn't have gone into the animal business.

When I told a veterinarian friend I had worked with previously what had gone on at several jobs, she said, "I've worked beside you for years. I *know* that doesn't describe you. Being told all those horrible things is why people are going home and shooting themselves. I'm surprised you're still here after all you've been through." This was coming from someone who was once so wrapped up in her identity as a veterinarian that she couldn't handle the loss of a dear patient in her care. She was supposed to help pets get better, not watch them die. Heartbreakingly, she did attempt to shoot herself, but by some divine intervention, the gun jammed. She openly shared her story with me, and it is profound in how it highlights the perfectionistic culture in which many of us work. We have to find healthy ways to cope with all the stress and nonsense, and it starts in our own minds. It's been a long road for each of us, but thankfully we have both found our ways of enduring. It's always a work in progress—some days are better than others. We now both have satisfying lives and a connection to a higher power. We have established boundaries at work and have fulfilling interests outside of our jobs, and we know how much the animals need our expertise and care. We know that we can't save them all, and we can't die trying. We're both living proof that it is possible to move on and find peace and purpose in the stressful world of veterinary medicine.

I believe that my current job does well in boosting morale on a regular basis. Sometimes it's the little things that have a huge impact on maintaining a cohesive team and a positive culture. We are provided with coffee, snacks, and even an amazing ice machine. Our bosses go out of their way to celebrate Vet Tech Week and all kinds of holidays. During important sporting events (March Madness, the World Cup, the Olympics), we have the large-screen TV on in the treatment area. On occasion we have food trucks bring us lunch or snacks. We participate in team-building activities such as the NeuroColor Temperament Inventory test and the DISC personality test. This is supposed to help us better understand our coworkers and how to relate to them on their terms. The Golden Rule (treat others how *you* wish to be treated) has now been replaced by the Platinum Rule (treat others how *they* wish to be treated). This requires having an awareness of someone besides yourself and your own outlook. Every Christmas, we have a staff party at the owner's house, with a huge dinner and gifts provided. During the pandemic we had a cooking class via Zoom and still got a chance to eat together, albeit virtually. Everyone gets a cake and card on their birthday. They try to give everyone a half-day morning shift followed by a full day off (this break can really help with recovering physically and mentally). We all laugh hard and often, and the jokes flow freely. This really helps us bond as a team and alleviate the daily stressors, especially because our bosses are usually right in the thick of it, if not leading the charge. Every staff meeting ends positively, with the manager reading thank-you notes that the staff write to one another when we're observed going above and beyond. If we have enough space available, the staff is allowed to bring their personal dogs to work. We all enjoy seeing them play together and help each other out with walking and feeding if necessary. Every January, we randomly draw names of staff members who want to participate in Secret Pal, where we anonymously buy our pal gifts throughout the year. The Secret Pal is revealed at the Christmas Party. If morale boosters aren't the norm at your clinic, maybe you can be the one to implement a few. Even a genuine smile or "Good morning!" instead of your usual grunt in their general direction can make someone's day. Remember the same thing when you're leaving for the day—saying goodbye and good job to your coworkers isn't that difficult. With small steps, working together, we can change the culture and create a wave of wellness.

## CHAPTER 5 TAKEAWAYS

1. Who controls the culture at your workplace? Are they open to hearing ways of doing things differently?

2. What can you contribute to raise the vibe?

3. Have you ever been treated with total disrespect by someone in authority? How did it make you feel? How could you have handled it differently?

## RESOURCES

* *The Gaslighting Recovery Workbook: Healing from Emotional Abuse* by Amy Marlow-MaCoy
* *Take Control of Your Life* by Mel Robbins
* *Dare To Lead* by Brené Brown
* *Daring Greatly* by Brené Brown
* *The Asshole Survival Guide: How to Deal with People Who Treat You Like Dirt* by Robert I. Sutton
* *10% Happier* by Dan Harris
* *Real Happiness at Work* by Sharon Salzberg

# PART TWO: THE MIND

*"Our life is shaped by our mind; we become what we think. Joy follows a pure thought like a shadow that never leaves."*

—Buddha

## CHAPTER 6: MINDFULNESS AND MEDITATION

One of the best things I discovered to help keep my sanity was meditation, because the stillness within brought many things to light. It's in the stillness that we find ourselves. So many people think they can't meditate because they can't clear their minds; these are the ones who need it the most. It's not about *not* thinking. Your heart beats, your lungs breathe, and your mind thinks, nonstop. However, just as you can slow down your heart rate and your breathing, you can slow down your thoughts. It's about coming back to an anchor, whether that's your breath or a mantra (a word or phrase you repeat over and over). Think of it like training a puppy to go to the bathroom outside. You bring her to the same spot over and over without judgment, and eventually you have a housebroken dog! Or think of your thoughts like clouds passing by—just let them drift and observe. If you start to focus on one because it reminds you of Mickey Mouse's head, notice that and bring your mind back to its anchor point. You WILL have thoughts. Lots of them. *This position is uncomfortable. My hand itches. What should I eat for dinner? Do you believe that asshole cut in front of me in line at the grocery store? Aww, my cat is so cute!* Try to make it more like this: *This position is so . . . breathe in, breathe out . . . My hand . . . breathe in, breathe out, breathe in . . . What should I eat . . . breathe in, breathe out, breathe in, breathe out.* Set a timer. Try to make this a mini habit— something you do for such a short amount of time that it's almost impossible *not* to do. This gets the momentum going, and you're more likely to stick with it. Meditate for just two minutes. Then five. It has been scientifically proven that even ten minutes a day can have powerful positive effects on the brain. Eventually work up to twenty or thirty minutes, once or twice a day. Some apps I really enjoy are Headspace and Insight Timer—both have guided meditations and courses.

Sit up straight, so the positive energy can flow through your body. This doesn't have to involve the full lotus position (seated with legs crossed and feet resting on your knees), like you've seen meditation gurus or Buddhist monks do. Just make sure you are comfortable, so you can relax and concentrate. There are meditation cushions, mats, and benches you can buy, but you don't need any special equipment. If you tend to get drowsy (which I do), try a walking meditation, slowly and consciously. I personally prefer guided meditations. It is easier for me to relax and escape when I can visualize walking on a sun-warmed beach with water lapping at my ankles or a fragrant pine-needle path through a forest. See what works best for you. The goal is to relax and give your mind a much-needed respite from all the internal chatter. One fun technique I use is to picture a cute monkey swinging from tree to tree, chattering away. I tell him (or her) to come to me and sit quietly for just a little while, so I can transition from *monkey mind* to *monk mind*, clearing away the cobwebs and clutter. You can imagine yourself sitting on a mountaintop, where you are above the clouds and see only blue sky. Or underwater where it is calm, away from all the waves and turbulence of the ocean. See each fish that swims by as one of your thoughts, and just observe them, without getting involved. This is by no means easy, but use your imagination and create your own world of serenity, an inner place you can always visit when the outside world gets to be too much.

*Breathwork* is also highly effective at calming our minds. There are many types of exercises, but I prefer to stick to simple ones I can do on the spur of the moment. Breathe in positive words, and breathe out negative ones—breathe in "stillness," breathe out "reactive." Breathe in "acceptance," breathe out "suffering." Breathe in "serenity," breathe out "chaos." Come up with your own list of words or phrases. As you will see, the benefits of meditation and conscious breathing far outweigh the struggle. You can also breathe in healing light and breathe out toxicity. Close your eyes and start with a deep, cleansing breath. Imagine breathing in a bright white light and breathing out black smoke. Take another breath of white light, and breathe out dark gray smoke. Another breath of white light before breathing out light gray smoke. Do this as many times as you want until you are breathing in *and* out a bright white, healing light. Feel it warming and illuminating your body and spreading beyond you into the world. Imagine family members, friends, or animals being near you and soaking up your healthy, healing energy. There are many forms of breathwork, and if you've ever practiced yoga, you may be familiar with several of them.

*Mindfulness* is the awareness of all that is around you. While it is best utilized during meditation, you can be mindful anywhere. Be mindful of your posture, be mindful of what or how fast you eat, be mindful when driving. Just try to be aware of your surroundings and be in the moment. This is not as easy as it may sound, believe me. The more I try to be mindful, the more difficult it seems! I set an intention to be mindful of what I eat during the day, and the next thing I know, I've inhaled several cookies. It's especially difficult in a fast-paced medical setting, when you're often doing multiple tasks at the same time with another twelve on the list. Try to at least be mindful of positive interactions throughout the day, and show gratitude for them. Being aware and giving someone your full attention is a gift. A silent "thank-you" for all the good things throughout the day helps bolster positive feelings. *"The mind reflects the world, and the world reflects the mind" (James Pierce).*

## CHAPTER 6 TAKEAWAYS

1. Make a commitment to at least start a mini habit for a few minutes of quiet time.

2. Did you live in the present today? Were you aware of moments of *now*, in which you weren't reminiscing about the past or worried about the future?

3. What or who are you grateful for today? List five things before going to bed tonight. Be grateful for

what is in your life *now*, not what you lost or what you wish you had.

## RESOURCES

* Insight Timer app
* Headspace app
* *8 Minute Meditation* by Victor Davich
* *The Headspace Guide to Meditation & Mindfulness* by Andy Puddicombe
* *Think Like a Monk* by Jay Shetty
* *The Power of Now* by Eckhart Tolle
* *Mini Habits: Smaller Habits, Bigger Results* by Stephen Guise

# CHAPTER 7:
# SIMPLICITY AND JOYFUL LIVING

Clutter infiltrates every aspect of our lives. It starts in our minds with unconscious negative talk about how we aren't good enough and gradually leaks out to affect our physical surroundings. As within, so without. Look at your environment through the eyes of a guest in your home. Would you be embarrassed to have unexpected company, or are you confident that your level of orderliness wouldn't raise eyebrows? Would you be ashamed if someone could read your mind? Are you your own worst enemy? Once you start to focus on the present and on calming your mind (dusting those mental cobwebs), you will realize the consequences of your mental clutter.

To have a simpler lifestyle, you need to pare down some of your belongings. Just like friends, objects can be here for a reason, a season, or a lifetime. Not everyone or everything deserves lifetime status. I like to combine the Buddhist philosophy of nonattachment with Marie Kondo's question, "Does it spark joy?" (I recommend her book *The Life-Changing Magic of Tidying Up*). Basically, her method entails holding an object, such as a piece of clothing or a book, one item at a time, and noticing whether it sparks joy within your body. If it makes you happy, keep it. If not, thank it for its service and let it go. You can donate it, sell it, recycle it, or throw it away. This is also true of gifts. Once the giver has passed on their present, it is out of their hands and none of their business what the recipient does with it. The true gift was in the giving. Be grateful, and if it doesn't suit you, thank it and pass it on to someone who *will* appreciate it. Wouldn't it be liberating if you didn't have to break out the crocheted doilies every time grandma came to visit?

When you clear space both mentally and physically, you can breathe a deep sigh of relief. The very air around you will feel lighter and be infused with joy. Getting rid of physical belongings can be extra difficult, as oftentimes there is significant emotional attachment. It is important to remember that the memories are stored within you, not in the object. Memories are of the past. What makes you happy *now?* Take your favorite blue shirt, for example, the one you wore on your first date with your now-husband, when he commented on how the color made your eyes look so pretty. Now hand that same shirt to a complete stranger, and they see . . . a blue shirt. That's it. No warm and fuzzy feelings of sentimentality. Obviously, this doesn't mean get rid of everything, but try to surround yourself only with things that make you happy in the present time.

Another concept that has to do with minimalism and simplifying to embrace mindful living is the Danish approach called *hygge* (pronounced hoog-uh), which essentially translates to *wholesome wellness.* The mindset is to see the bright and happy in all things, listen, and be present. It also invokes the Nordic culture of getting out into nature and bringing nature indoors. It's about making the winter months more enjoyable by wearing warm, comfortable clothes and surrounding yourself with firelight, candles, good books, music, hot chocolate, and the people you love. They have a saying: "There is no bad weather, only bad clothing." Keep things simple, and, like

Danish society, focus on people and relationships, coziness and contentment, not material things. Enjoy the seasons as they come around, and look for positive things in the ones that aren't your favorite. I used to despise the winter months, but now I look forward to them as a time to relax and recover. I enjoy the magic of the holiday season and look forward to snow days by the fire, sipping hot chocolate. Some people despise the heat of summer, but can you appreciate the lushness of the trees, the happy chirping of birds, and the nighttime symphony of tree frogs? Your happiness is a choice in any situation. *"Everything can be taken from a man but one thing: the last of the human freedoms—to choose one's attitude in any given set of circumstances, to choose one's own way"* (Viktor Frankl).

To avoid becoming overly attached to my belongings, I acknowledge that everything in our existence is transient. I don't truly own my house, any more than the previous residents did. I deeply love my house and property, but I am a caretaker and steward entrusted with it while it is in my possession. It will be here when I am gone, entrusted to the next caretakers. Nor do I own my animals in that way—they are a precious gift to share my life with, for as long as that may be. This doesn't mean I love them any less or grieve their loss any differently, but I try to appreciate them more and am perhaps more tolerant of their shortcomings. We are all on borrowed time, and I have made peace with that to the best of my ability.

I learned this lesson of borrowed time the hard way. My beloved American Foxhound, Zoe, was my soul dog. We had a somewhat rough start, as she was my first puppy, and I wasn't prepared for having my belongings chewed up. A defining moment arrived when I got really upset at something important she had chewed up, and I yelled at her. I am not proud of that moment, and I was saddened by the fact that she hid from me for the rest of that day. I finally sought her out and asked her, calmly, if we could please be friends. After that we were inseparable soul mates. One day about seven years later, I was sitting on the sofa with her, watching my brand-new TV. I distinctly remember thinking *I pray that she lives another ten years. I love this dog so much!* She was dead ten hours later. I took her to work with me on a horse farm like always, and for some unknown reason she ran across the street and was struck by a truck. The man who hit her stopped and left me his phone number. He felt terrible. I was devastated. Instead of screaming at him, I remained calm and thanked him for stopping. I knew it had been an accident. *There is much power in forgiveness.* Although we rushed her to the emergency hospital, I knew on the way there that she couldn't be saved. It was a struggle between my rational vet tech mind and my emotional mommy mind as I listened to her last breaths. There were several horses and dogs buried on the property of the farm where I worked, and because Zoe loved it out there so much, I asked if I could bury her in the back pasture. The owner said, "I can hand you a shovel," even though I knew he had the proper equipment to make this an easy task. Yet another person with no empathy. I ended up taking her to work and placing her in the freezer myself to be cremated later. I cried for days. My coworkers and boyfriend were also deeply hurt by her loss. One day when I was home grieving, I looked up at the sky, and just then the tree branches parted to form a cross of blue sky. I grabbed my camera and snapped a picture, just before it morphed into the shape of a dove. I knew in my heart it was a sign that she was at peace. Several weeks later, I had a vivid dream about her, which many would consider a visitation. She was at a vet office, completely whole and healthy. She ran to me and jumped in my arms, and I wrapped myself around her warm, wiggly body. I said, "I love you!" and she replied, in plain English, "I know." It was a defining moment for me, one in which I realized that the material stuff doesn't matter in the long run.

What matters is relationships and the love surrounding them. Life is short and fragile and unpredictable. Remind yourself that you are living "the good ol' days" right now, and don't let the past or future hijack your experience. Surround yourself with beauty and love, and be grateful for what you have, instead of pining away for what you want. Clear the mental cobwebs and physical clutter, and *choose* your perspective from a place of clarity and joy. Make sure you are living your life in accordance with your values. Schedule time off on occasion to reset and have quality time with the ones you love. Having a set routine can help keep you on track.

## CHAPTER 7 TAKEAWAYS

1. What sparked joy in you today?

2. What outdated mental clutter did you choose to release and not focus on?

3. What material objects are you okay with letting go of to make space for peace?

4. Did you spend quality time with your family and

pets today? (This means without an electronic device in your hand.) Did you really listen and pay attention?

5. Are you actually valuing what you say is important to you? Are you spending time on your computer or at work over family time? Don't work so hard at earning a living that your spouse and children only get your leftover energy.

## RESOURCES

* *The Life-Changing Magic of Tidying Up* by Marie Kondo
* *American Hygge* by Melanie Morgan
* *Simply Clean* by Becky Rapinchuk (founder of Clean Mama website)
* *Let It Go: Downsizing Your Way to a Richer, Happier Life* by Peter Walsh
* *Enough Already! Clearing Mental Clutter to Become the Best You* by Peter Walsh

# CHAPTER 8: RITUAL AND ROUTINE

Having a routine gives us an anchor point—a plan and a purpose for our day. Some see a routine as another chore to cross off the list, but it doesn't have to be viewed that way. There is scientific evidence that using an early morning routine has positive effects on productivity. Many successful people rise hours earlier than the general population to get started on their day, ahead of the competition.

A ritual is a set of actions performed regularly. It doesn't necessarily have anything to do with religion, although there are many rituals associated with that. Many of us view morning coffee as a ritual. Here is an opportunity to be mindful as well. From choosing your mug to picking out a flavor, smelling the aroma of those first drops, and listening to the percolating, it's something we look forward to. So pour yourself that "cup of ambition," as Dolly Parton sings in "9-to-5," and get on with your day. Personally, before I have my coffee, I drink a glass of my "morning mocktail," which is a flavored water that I keep on my nightstand. A brand called Early Bird makes a special blend to help you wake up—you make it in a cocktail shaker the night before. It's a fun ritual, and it ensures I drink water upon waking. The other brand I use is Liquid IV, which contains electrolytes.

Before the day takes control of you, carve out time for yourself. Before the kids get up and the dog wants to go out, have your own quiet space. I was inspired by Hal

Elrod's book *The Miracle Morning*—a routine that includes silence (meditation or prayer), positive affirmations, visualization about how you want your day to go, exercise, reading, and writing. You do each of these for a set amount of time, which lays the groundwork for the rest of your day. It's much better than hitting snooze multiple times, skipping breakfast, running around forgetting things, and stressing out the entire family in a rush to get out the door. Some hustle is needed to be on time in the morning, but feeling chaotic isn't necessary. Parkinson's Law states that "work expands so as to fill the time available for its completion." I have found this to be very true of my mornings. No matter how much extra time I gave myself, tasks seemed to fill the space until I was rushing out the door anyway. I now try to be more mindful and plan accordingly.

I use a sunrise alarm clock, which gradually brightens from deep red to sunny yellow over about thirty minutes (Hatch, hOmeLabs, and Phillips are recommended brands). For a sensitive person, this is a blessing, as bright lights and loud noises set our nervous systems on edge. After the subtle alarm of birds chirping or ocean waves crashing, I chug my morning mocktail and make my way downstairs for coffee. Don't turn on the television or look at your phone for at least fifteen minutes. When your brain is still hazy, the news negativity imprints on it and can contribute to a pessimistic feeling all day. Instead I put on music, or more likely, an uplifting podcast. A few I recommend are *On Purpose* with Jay Shetty, *Essential Teachings* with Eckhart Tolle, *Achieve Your Goals* with Hal Elrod, and *The Highest Self Podcast* with Sahara Rose. Find what resonates with you. Sometimes I just enjoy my coffee while watching the sun come up and the birds visit my feeders, and other times I do the full Miracle Morning routine, depending on how much time I have. Have a routine of waking your kids up in a positive way. (Please don't loudly play a fake trumpet in their doorway, which is how I was woken up on occasion. Highly sensitive people especially don't like this.) Get up early enough to help your spouse, so their day goes better. Ask what you can do for them today. Make small changes a habit, and the results will snowball. Be sure to make your bed before leaving the house—this will set up your nighttime routine. Hopefully this will create a peaceful and positive running start to your day.

What about the rest of your day? Here is where being mindful of your thoughts as often as possible can be useful. Throughout the day, I often stop to take a deep cleansing breath or check in with myself. (However, my deep breaths have been misconstrued as huge sighs and me being "negative and stressed out," which then led to a manager having a talk with me about my "attitude.") Focus briefly on something near you, so you can be grounded in the moment. Notice how soft the puppy's fur is. Smell the coffee brewing in the breakroom. Listen to the phones ringing. Observe the bright colors of your coworker's scrub top. Just be present and enjoy the moment with no judgment. A good exercise if you're feeling anxious is to focus on five things you can see, four things you can touch, three things you can hear, two things you can smell, and one thing you can taste in your environment (those last two may be dicey in a veterinary clinic). This will bring your mind to the present, so it has something to anchor to other than its usual hamster wheel worry loop.

Some good little habits to sprinkle throughout your day might also include meditating for two minutes, drinking a few sips of water, stretching your back and legs, and saying something kind to a peer or client. Remember, the point of a mini habit is to do something so small that you can't *not* do it, but once you get the momentum going, you will most likely continue. Who's really going to get on the floor for only one push-up? Or drink only one sip of water? If you promise yourself that you only have to do the minimum goal you set, you can never fail and will usually surpass your goal. I admittedly struggle with remembering to do these things, as I think anyone in the medical field can relate to. Make it a routine, and you will see improvement. During the winter months, use a "happy lamp" at your desk, such as Verilux brand, which uses clinically proven full-spectrum light to enhance your mood.

To end the day on a positive note, it's important to have a nighttime ritual. It's what sets you up for your successful morning. Cut back on the caffeine or alcohol or sweets (or whatever vice you have). Make your bedroom a peaceful retreat, with low clutter and soothing colors. If you made your bed in the morning, it will be much more inviting to crawl between your sheets. Put the phone and other electronic devices away at least thirty minutes before falling asleep. I promise, the world won't end before you wake up, and if it does, there was nothing you could have done about it anyway. Cover up any ambient light, especially blue light, coming from equipment such as DVRs, fans, air purifiers, humidifiers, etc. (I use black electrical tape, because any stray light keeps me awake.) Have a good skincare routine to make you feel pampered. Take a bath or shower before bed to wash the day off. Or you can try *Kenyoko*, the Japanese word for "dry bathing." It is said to purify the body and soul, and it is often used before entering sacred spaces. Place your right hand on your left shoulder and brush down across your chest and stomach, ending at your right hip. Repeat with your other hand. Do this twice, and then fling your hand away from your body, as if you are throwing away any negative energy for the earth to recycle. (You can do this after leaving work, to make a physical and mental transition.) Sometimes I burn sage leaves to dispel any negativity. Drink some soothing tea, such as Kava Stress Relief, and read an inspiring book or an escapist novel. Write down your thoughts or concerns in a journal to get them out of your head. Balance this with writing a few specific things you were grateful for today. Dab a calming essential oil, such as lavender or chamomile, on your wrists or the bottoms of your feet. Don't forget to prepare your morning mocktail and put it on your nightstand. Let your mind and body rest for at least seven to eight hours, so you'll have a positive start for whatever tomorrow throws at you. Sweet dreams!

## CHAPTER 8 TAKEAWAYS

1. How can you ensure you will get up earlier tomorrow to get a positive start on your day?

2. Which morning or nighttime rituals resonate with you?

3. How can you carve out moments of peace in your hectic day?

4. Name five specific things that you were grateful for today.

## RESOURCES

* *The Miracle Morning* by Hal Elrod
* *The Miracle Equation* by Hal Elrod
* *High Performance Habits* by Brendon Burchard
* *Mind Over Mood* by Dennis Greenberger, PhD and Christine Padesky, PhD

# PART THREE: THE BODY

*"For you formed my inward parts; you knitted me together in my mother's womb. I praise you, for I am fearfully and wonderfully made. Wonderful are your works; my soul knows it very well."*

—Psalm 139:13–14

Each of us is a soul housed within a vessel we call the body. That soul is pure life-force energy. It is the intelligent, formless, and timeless dimension that animates every living thing. It is the unpolluted essence that is our birthright. But then outside influences start to taint us, and the polluted mind takes over. Soon we are polluting our bodies as well. Not everyone is happy with the vessel they've been allotted in this lifetime. But if we think of it as God's (or Source's) gift to us, we can be appreciative of the lessons it has to teach us. If we received a gift from a dear friend, would we look at it critically, then hand it back and say "Thanks, but it's too big . . . It's the wrong color . . . It's too small . . . This part over here isn't quite perfect"? Probably not, yet we judge, analyze, critique, and dismiss the ultimate gift, our own body, all the time. In this section we will try to see this sacred vessel for what it is and honor it with exercise, nutrition, and pampering. As medical personnel, we witness the miracle of the body every day in the animals we care for. We see the difference that proper care makes in the healing process, as well as in daily mental and physical health. Yet when it comes to ourselves, we often abuse and neglect that aspect of self-care. Let's try to change that!

# CHAPTER 9: BURNOUT AND STRESS

I've already discussed a few areas that can cause burnout, such as a pervasively toxic culture, poor nutrition, a lack of mental or physical breaks during a workday, and no time or energy for exercising. I told you about my professional "why" earlier in the book. Think about yours again, and make it your anchor in stormy seas. While some of what I write next may apply mainly to veterinarians and technicians, other staff members absolutely feel the anxiety and emotional pain of the job. In what was once a male-dominated profession, females currently make up 80% of students enrolled in vet school. Add to that the other burdens that females typically shoulder, such as raising a family and taking care of the household, and there is an even higher rate of burnout, stress, and suicide. Those with a degree who think of this as their career may have a more vested interest in sticking it out, while there is a higher turnover rate for other staff members, who consider this job a stepping-stone and get the heck out as soon as something more profitable or less stressful comes along. Don't forget the physical pain: being constantly covered in scratches and bruises isn't exactly fun. It is far from an easy road, yet it can be a very rewarding one. At least it's rarely boring! Learn to seek out and focus on all the positives throughout the day: the cute puppies, the wonderful clients, the coworkers you enjoy, the animals you helped. Keep a journal of all your victories or a scrapbook with the notes and cards from clients who are grateful for your work. Refer to these whenever you're feeling down.

You probably hit the ground running, and you're lucky if you get a lunch or bathroom break. Many of us don't get to sit down during a shift, much less get any mental rest. As previously mentioned, the breakroom is full of cookies and donuts, which you grab on the run because you think it's better than not eating anything. By midweek you're longing for a vegetable tray and wondering why your pants don't fit. At one job, I actually bought a pack of cigarettes, just so I would be allowed to have a break like the others. I would get fussed at for sitting down for five minutes, while several coworkers were on their fifth smoking break of the day. You have to fight for a culture that's fair and inclusive. You arrive home after a ten or twelve-hour shift, mentally exhausted from figuring out cases and worrying about your patients, with your legs so tired from rushing around that they actually cramp in the middle of the night. You still have to carve out quality time with your family and your own pets, even though you're hungry and in pain and tired beyond reason. You're probably suffering from decision fatigue as well and feel like a mental zombie.

Burning out loyal employees has never made a lick of sense to me. If you're sensitive like me, you're energetically drained as well from taking on everyone else's emotions and moods. I'd been to several doctors, explaining how exhausted I was all the time, and all they did was say that my tests were normal and suggest putting me on antidepressants. Not one of them looked beyond my physical presentation to what could be the *cause.* No one took the time to listen to my concerns and get to the root of the problem. This has become your average Western-based, ten-minute consult: here's some pills! Get 'em in, get 'em out ("treat and street")! Remember, if you *need* medication, then by all means take it. But at that particular time, I didn't feel mentally depressed. I *wanted* to go outside and enjoy the sunshine—it was just a huge physical effort. I was so groggy half the time that I could barely keep my eyes open. When I became more mindful, I began to solve this problem on my own. I started to notice that the groggy feeling happened regularly around certain people. It still took me a while to realize that I was *energetically* drained from being an empath, and that it wasn't stemming from a physical problem. All the commotion, noise, talking, barking, drama, and hustle at your average vet clinic is very taxing to the nervous system. Add to that the behind-the-scenes bullying, gaslighting, and snubbing, and it's a wonder we show up to do it all again the next day. This profession is a calling, and we do it out of love and devotion for the animals in our care.

Did you start off as a bright flame, burning to make a difference in the profession? Perhaps you were a new grad with high expectations about serving clients who are grateful for your knowledge, helping their sick pets get well, and balancing a happy family life. But then at some point, the hard truth started to seep in and dampen your flame. You realized you can't fix all your patients, and perhaps impostor syndrome crept in. You start to think you're not good enough at this. Did you even learn some of this stuff in school? Were you out sick the day they covered *that?* Are your peers tired of you constantly asking them questions? How are you going to tell Mrs. Smith that her beloved golden retriever has lymphoma? After all, her husband died recently, and Bella is all she has. Why can't you get Mr. Thomas's cat to stop vomiting? You've taken X-rays, done bloodwork, performed an ultrasound, switched her food, and tried several medications. These cases are just a few of the dozens you've seen this week, and it's only Tuesday afternoon. With the unexpected pet boom during the pandemic, you have far more cases than you can handle, as do all of your colleagues. You're not sure you can handle one more over-rambunctious, untrained, "fur baby" Doodle-something (Snickerdoodles, Barkadoodles, Whackadoodles . . . but I digress). Your coworkers are always having some sort of drama, but the manager shrugs it off (you're too sensitive, after all). If you have to hear about Julie's on-again, off-again ex-boyfriend one more time! Or try to escape from someone else's constant attention-seeking behavior—there are only so many places to hide for a minute. It's exhausting. You might start to feel like a burning matchstick, with the flame dying down and the beginning of some char. You're just plain tired, at work and at home. Until you get used to it, the daily uncertainty of what's going to walk through the clinic doors, while exciting, can also leave you immersed in fear. We are all a superstitious bunch, and most of us know better than to speak aloud such unmentionables as "Boy it sure is quiet today" or "That looks like a really good vein!" Are you wondering whether this was the right career choice after all? Once you've been employed for a while, you may become more confident in your abilities, although you swiftly find out that clients think "Dr. Google" knows more than you, as do their breeder, groomer, and neighbor. You may start to feel resentful of the demanding clients who tell you you're just in it for the money (we can all have a good belly laugh here before we leave in our Lamborghinis) because you won't do a discounted exam for their *rescue dog.* You have sacrificed your personal time to research problems and call clients after-hours when no one seems appreciative. *"What is to give light must endure burning."* (Viktor Frankl)

Coworkers and leaders aren't the only source of bullying in the workplace. Clients can be some of the biggest bullies, and they tend to prey on those they think are the weakest link, such as the front desk staff and assistants trying to get a medical history on their pet. They will manipulate, bully, and intimidate their way to paying less for services. Keep in mind that this behavior is usually a result of their own issues around their financial situation and not a reflection of your professional services. They are probably like this with all service industry personnel. Acting indignant deflects their feelings around their own insecurities. Rarely will they be so rude to the veterinarian. It blows my mind that people will pay $7000 for a "purebred" designer mutt, yet complain about the cost of spaying them. Compared to the actual cost of a human hysterectomy, they're getting quite a deal! Clients often don't make the connection that they have *health insurance* that pays for most of their personal medical costs, whereas vet clinics and their clients have to absorb those costs themselves. I'm also not quite sure where they come up with the prices they consider "reasonable," such as, "I thought the dental was going to be $200!" Really? In what world does bloodwork, a catheter, anesthesia, fluids, an ECG and other monitoring equipment, a licensed technician to clean and polish, and multiple extractions that took two hours only cost $200? Another favorite is "I thought insulin only cost $30! This is preposterous!" But I'm preaching to the choir—I'm sure many of you have clients like this. Nothing is ever right: your prices are too high, the receptionist was rude, the medications weren't ready on time, they had to wait five minutes to be seen, which is completely unacceptable to them, and you can't ever diagnose their pet properly. Yet they keep coming back, year after year. That's because it's not really you that's the problem— it's them. I can think of a few clients in particular who always, every single visit, treat the staff in a despicable manner, including cursing at them. When this is brought to their attention, they typically deny and deflect, acting as if they have no idea what you're talking about. They can be truly clueless, unless they're narcissistic and thrive off negativity and pain. I honestly believe that some people walk through life unconscious of their own energy and actions. I also believe there are those who live to deceive and control others. Either way, it's unacceptable behavior that needs to be brought into the light of day and not tolerated. Why we continue to cater to these people is beyond me. I heard of a vet clinic that has a meeting once a year, at which the entire staff gets to vote on up to three clients to fire. I think this empowers everyone to be allowed the dignity of being treated with respect.

Effectively communicating with and actively listening to our clients and team members can go a long way toward avoiding conflict in the first place. We must try to keep in mind that there are many different communication styles, especially between the different generations we see as clients. Does your hospital have a policy in place for using proper tone, empathy, politeness, and common slang? Saying "That's off the chain, dude!" may not be the best approach when speaking to someone with gray hair. An example of miscommunication that stands out in my mind is a lady who brought her cat in and told the receptionist she was being "put to sleep." The receptionist assumed this meant euthanasia, but what the client actually meant was that her cat was being *sedated* to be groomed! Luckily this was sorted out and ended well, due to rigorous checks and balances. Another example is when a vet told a tech to "be sure to shave the right leg," which she did. What he meant was to shave the *correct* leg, which happened to be the left. Likewise, use correct units of measure, and be sure your clients understand them. When dealing with insulin, for example, if a client incorrectly tells a neighbor or friend who is pet sitting to give the pet 3 *mls* instead of 3 *units*, it may not end well, depending on their level of knowledge. When telling an owner to give 0.05 mls, make sure they realize it's not 0.5 mls. In medicine, we must be very aware of the terms we use with each other and with clients.

If you commiserate with your peers to communicate your unhappiness, that can also contribute to a complaining culture, whether or not that's your intention. Especially for females, this can be a way to vent and connect with each other, but it may not always be seen that way. Been there, done that. Years ago, several of us were talking about an unfair situation at work when the boss walked into the room. He looked right at me and demanded, "What did you just say?" Everyone else in the room scattered like roaches, and I was left alone to make a split-second decision. I looked my boss straight in the eye and told him the truth about the culture there, what the complaints were, and that he needed to listen instead of yelling and walking away, or in a few cases, firing the complainer. Luckily, the vet who was next in charge walked into that confrontation and confirmed what I was saying. The boss listened to her and to me, then squeezed my shoulder and told me it was going to be okay. From that day on, my boss had a new level of respect for me. It doesn't always turn out well when I speak my truth, but that time it did because he took the time to interact instead of react, and I had someone willing to back me up. I hate to break the news, but the person complaining is usually just a scapegoat for a far greater culture issue. They're like the canary in the coal mine, and getting rid of every canary won't fix what's making them sick. Get rid of the loudest canary before it dies on your watch, and there's soon another to take its place, because it's the toxic air that's killing them, not the loudness of their voice desperately seeking help. We need leaders who *hear* us and take action on our behalf.

Some of you may no longer enjoy your day off because you know you'll have anxiety and worrisome thoughts about going back to work and the uncertainty of what you might face. We may start to find unhealthy ways to cope with the stress. Cue the donuts in the breakroom, the afternoon coffee or Red Bull, the binge-watching TV with a glass of wine and bag of chips once we're home. A few peers I've known over the years have used far more toxic things to cope, which never ends well. We worry about our patients and may stay up late researching and brainstorming. We now have to worry about bullying and bad reviews on social media, which adds another layer of stress. Unfortunately, in today's culture, one misunderstanding can lead to a negative pack mentality on the internet, even when the majority of the naysayers have no idea what the situation was about. Our significant others may not understand why we're so zoned out most of the time. At this stage in the game, you may just be char and wisps of smoke, but I hope I have given you valid suggestions on how to make your flame smolder again and eventually burn bright, so you can illuminate others' paths as well as your own.

Self-care is not selfish, it is essential. It is nonnegotiable. You must tend to your burned-out self.

## CHAPTER 9 TAKEAWAYS

1. What action steps can you take to avoid burnout?

2. What do you do for self-care? How often?

3. How can you separate client or coworker rudeness from a personal attack?

4. What tools have you incorporated so far? Meditation? Having a morning ritual? Remembering your *why* for being where you are? Conjuring up an alter ego to give you more confidence? Remember, *action* is needed to make a difference in your life!

## RESOURCES

* *A Radical Awakening: Turn Pain into Power, Embrace Your Truth, Live Free* by Dr. Shefali Tsabary
* *Your Time to Thrive: End Burnout, Increase Well-being* by Marina Khidekel
* *The Tapping Solution* by Nick Ortner
* *A Complaint Free World* by Will Bowen
* *Life Code* by Dr. Phil McGraw
* *Becoming Supernatural* by Dr. Joe Dispenza
* *The Emotion Code* by Dr. Bradley Nelson

# CHAPTER 10: EXERCISE AND NUTRITION

## EXERCISE

Ugh. End of chapter. Yup, that pretty much sums up my feelings about the word *exercise.* Yet we all know we need it. We all know we should do it. We all know the benefits. I'm sure I'm not alone in feeling that after walking a few miles around the clinic all day, lifting heavy animals, and wrestling on the floor with less-than-cooperative patients, the thought of having to go home and *exercise* is daunting. It sounds like one more chore to get done. Maybe that's because I equate that word with jogging, spin class, aerobics, and weight lifting—none of which bring me an ounce of joy. But hey, if that's your thing, that's great! Know that I admire you! My story about training for a 5K ended on Day 1. I was using the Couch to 5K app, diligently following instructions as I walked and jogged, walked and jogged, walked and jogged on some nearby trails around a lake. Finally, just when I was getting really winded, the lady giving instructions said, "Congratulations!" and I thought, *Okay, that wasn't so bad. I can do this.* "You're halfway done!" she finished, and I almost threw my phone in the lake.

I personally prefer to relabel the activity as something like "Let's move our chi," which aligns with my energy work and makes me more likely to move my body. (This is not to be confused with the book *Who Moved My Cheese?* by Spencer Johnson, MD, which I also recommend.) I prefer yoga, Tai Chi, hiking, kayaking, horseback riding, and taking the dogs on nature walks. Because I enjoy each of these activities, they don't seem like work to me, so it removes the negative connotation that I associate with exercise. If you have the fortitude to get up early and get it out of the way before your day overtakes you, that's probably best. I used to get up early and take the dogs on a walk before work. The problem was that my mainly outdoor cat used to follow us the entire way, and I became concerned for his safety. Sometimes I thought we had gotten away with sneaking out, only to have Ninja show up unexpectedly about a quarter mile in, meowing plaintively for us to slow down, so he could catch up. At times I would have to carry him home, which was not the type of exercise I had in mind. Even a ten-pound load gets heavier by the step, especially when you're trying to keep three dogs under control! Needless to say, our early morning canine excursions came to a halt. I now have to drive them to another location to avoid cat company.

I'm a horse person, and pretty much anything involved with them can count as exercise: grooming, cleaning stalls, hauling water buckets, lifting hay bales and fifty-pound feed bags, and of course, actual riding. Similarly, kayaking hardly seems like work to me because I'm too busy enjoying the water and birdwatching. Find something you enjoy that strengthens your muscles and gets your heart pumping. Getting out in nature can be fitness for the body *and* the soul.

## NUTRITION

Oh boy, another one of my least favorite topics. Not because I don't think it's important. On the contrary, it's probably one of the most important things you can do for your health. Much like exercise, I don't like the word *diet.* If you agree, come up with something more inspiring and lasting, such as *lifestyle change.* We all know fad diets don't work—you can't eat only grapefruits or never consume another carb. You have to find something sustainable over the long haul. I've always aspired to eat well and have mostly fallen short, I'm ashamed to admit. I can do well for a while—eating salads, cutting back on sugary drinks, eating fruits and vegetables regularly. But somehow the thought of a Dairy Queen Blizzard soon has me pulled back into the trenches of a sugar fix (which is apparently as addictive as cocaine). That's one of the main obstacles blocking my success: I love sweets. Especially chocolate. If the breakroom at your job is like most of the ones I've been in, it is laden with donuts, cupcakes, candy, cookies, bagels, and pizza. Am I right? And holidays are ten times worse, as well-meaning clients, staff members, and drug reps sweep in with daily goodies. We all know that we don't get regular lunch breaks in this business, so the lure of the sugar-shock breakroom pulls us in; it's almost impossible to resist the array of choices. It becomes an unconscious indulgence. The problem is, you then need to buy a larger scrub size every year, and no one wants that. There's always a large walk-on scale available in the clinic to chart your upward spiral and confirm your body image issues. All of these sugar- and preservative-laden nonfood items are devoid of any life-force energy—they are dead. This is pretty prevalent in dry pet kibble as well, but that's a whole other controversial topic. Asian cultures are very aware of the living energy in foods and how they affect the body. Study up on Traditional Chinese Veterinary Medicine (TCVM) to learn more. How are dead foods supposed to sustain and nourish us? These include boxed, packaged, canned, leftover, microwaved, and unnatural. All they do is make us sick and cause weight gain. I started feeling depressed about that a few years ago. Although I was "only" 135 pounds, I had a few clients ask me when I was expecting. One client interaction really sticks out in my mind. She brought in a litter of puppies for their second round of vaccines. I said, "They're getting so big!" and she pointed to my stomach and replied, "So are you!" I felt humiliated and ashamed. Add in a few more years and a slowing metabolism and, well, you get the picture that your bad habits need to be curbed sooner rather than later.

I now try to look at body image in terms of the Japanese phrase *wabi-sabi.* In a nutshell, it means understated beauty revealed through time, endurance, and age. It is the natural progression of life and all the imperfections that encompasses. This typically applies to such things as the green patina on copper, dents and scratches in an old wooden table, or the rusting of a metal roof. We see these "flaws" as aging beautifully with a story to tell, yet when we look in the mirror, all we see are our imperfections. It is an honor to have weathered the storms of life—your scars and wrinkles are just the patina that adds character. *We are all perfectly imperfect.*

I'm not one who can eat breakfast before 9:00 a.m., or I tend to get nauseated. I get up early to take care of my own animals, to pet sit, and to do my Miracle Morning when there's time. However, when you have to be at work by 7:30, and the pace is nonstop as soon as you walk in the door, it's hard to get a nutritious start to the day, and the negative effects just snowball from there. Before noon I'm usually getting weak and shaky, and as my coworker is fond of saying, my stomach walls are probably touching. Some days I may not get a break until 2:30 in the afternoon, and other days none at all. This seems to be part of the culture in any medical profession; I've personally never understood it. There's no valor in neglecting your own health while caring for the health of patients. Day after day, month after month, year after year, the effects accumulate.

As I've said earlier, I start my day with my morning mocktail, to which I usually add a powdered hydration boost or flavoring. This way I know that some water is allegedly getting into my cells instead of going right through me. Being properly hydrated can also help curb your appetite. (Do what I say here, not what I do.) I don't want to be a hypocrite, but anyone who knows me also knows how little water I actually drink. (I even went hiking in the desert and didn't think to bring water.) Who has time for a bathroom break at work anyway? In some states, regular breaks are not required by law, and when your day starts as the sun comes up and doesn't stop until it's dark outside, it's difficult to eat properly and remember to drink water. This is not health-sustaining in the long run. You have to be your own advocate, because the truth is, no one else is going to care about your long-term health. How many of us have gone to work exhausted or sick because we couldn't afford to take the day off, yet we're expected to work at our usual full steam ahead? There have been many times when I was sure that if I collapsed on the floor, people would just step over me. So what do we do about it?

- We can take high-quality vitamins to supplement our meals.

- We can make a protein shake or smoothie. I even buy premade ones such as

  Ensure or Boost, even though my coworkers make fun of me (they call me old).

- Incorporate a whole food supplement as a meal, such as Organifi or Ka'Chava.
- Bring a premixed salad to work. Add the dressing right before you eat it, so it doesn't become soggy. No one likes limp lettuce.
- Find a healthy replacement for sugary sodas. I've found that I love kombucha (fermented tea). It may be an acquired taste, but I now crave the refreshing zing in place of soda. Mojito lime mint coconut, anyone?
- Set a timer on your phone to be sure you're drinking enough water throughout the day.
- Keep unsalted nuts on hand for a healthy snack.
- Prep healthy meals in advance, so you don't have to think about it—just grab and go. There are now many options for meal delivery services as well.

Do what fits your schedule and personality, whether that's going all in on a lifestyle change or slowly incorporating new things until they become habits. None of this is one-size-fits-all, so do what works for you. Having a healthy mind and body is essential for combating stress in all areas of your life.

## CHAPTER 10 TAKEAWAYS

1. What habit can you tweak to make it healthier? Can it start out as a mini habit (just a few sips of water at a time)?

2. Did you carve out some personal time this week to exercise? Walking your dog around the block instead of just letting her out in the yard is a good start (remember to be mindful of the nature around you).

3. Identify your bad habits to bring them into your awareness. Don't forget to replace any bad habit with a positive one.

4. How are you perfectly imperfect, and how can you embrace that?

## RESOURCES

* *The Wabi-Sabi Way: Simple Principles to Bring Calm, Meaning, and Authenticity to Your Daily Life* by Mike Sturm
* *Mini Habits for Weight Loss* by Stephen Guise
* *Breaking Up with Sugar* by Molly Carmel
* *The Gifts of Imperfection* by Brené Brown, PhD

# PART FOUR: THE SPIRIT/SOUL

You are the *awareness* of all that you experience. You are the observer of your life.

## CHAPTER 11: BEING PRESENT AND AWARE

Existing in the present moment helps to quell the ego's insatiable thirst. Authentic, lasting happiness cannot be found outside of yourself. Societal cues such as TV commercials would like you to think otherwise. Your ego would like you to think otherwise, as it always wants more. More belongings, more relationships—it's never satisfied. Sure, material objects can make us all feel joy for a little while. But how long before that new outfit is old news, and your ego wants another one? How long before being in love turns into a rocky road, and you develop a roving eye? Despite what the movies want you to believe, someone else can't complete you (although it sure makes things smoother and easier if you have a compatible partner to share life with). Oftentimes the ego wants drama, so we ultimately create our own suffering. While this may not make logical sense, we see it all the time: the painful monster within that has gone through trauma needs to constantly be fed more pain. Have you known people (perhaps yourself) who are constantly negative, and nothing ever goes right for them? They overreact to every little slight, and their attitude toward life becomes a self-fulfilling prophecy. There are times I want to say, "Why would you expect anything different?" It's as if they walk around like gunslingers, looking to pick a fight with anyone and anything, yet we take it personally when they turn their sights on us. They create the storm, then get mad when lightning strikes. A major hurdle to happiness, known as suffering, is when we can't let go of the things we have no control over.

If there's truly no positive outcome to all your worry and anxiety, then you're just spinning your wheels in the mud and not going anywhere. (I know, I've had a lot of mud spattered on me.) Those of us who deal with anxiety know all about this. Before you spin out of control, take a deep breath. Imagine tree roots growing out of your feet and anchoring you to the earth. Be present. All of life is impermanent and transient—this, too, shall pass.

There is a gap, a small, sacred space of stillness, between your thoughts and your emotions. How you *feel* about things will then determine how you *act*. That small space gives you time to choose your behavior by consciously controlling what you're thinking. You don't have to react to every perceived slight—*you don't have to attend every party you're invited to.* No matter the subject, there are always those who try to remind you of how they are right and you are wrong. Remember what we learned about narcissists? These people are always looking for a reaction from you to engage their ego drama, and if you stop feeding into it, they will eventually go find other prey. You won't be fun to harass anymore. Which is fine, because you have better things to do with your time, like concentrating on creating your best possible life—living the highest version of your dreams.

Now you know the special trick of noticing the sacred space between your thinking and your emotional reaction to something, so you can *choose* the appropriate behavior. And it is a choice. Notice how your body physically reacts to your thoughts. Do you get butterflies in the stomach, sweating, shaking, shortness of breath? Do you feel yourself getting flustered, angry, frustrated, or otherwise upset? Is what you're thinking at that moment *actually true?* Are you sure? Or is it a story you've spun in your mind based on circumstances and your past conditioning? Does your coworker really hate you, or is she upset over something unrelated and just happened to snap at you? I'm sure we all know people who we wish had some sort of filter covering their mouth before unconsciously spewing out venom. Remember that we all have some sort of pain monster inside us that can be hard to control. It has its own agenda, which most hosts of this parasite aren't consciously aware of. Give it a name, an identity, so you can quickly notice its presence. (Oh no, Medusa is rearing her ugly head again!) It's not easy, but if you practice being aware of how your thoughts affect your actions, and therefore affect others, you'll live a more peaceful life by keeping your own monster sleeping in its den. I don't mean that you should suppress your feelings, just that you should be aware of them and the drama surrounding them.

Relinquishing control and being at peace with whatever is happening in the present moment is the only way to relieve suffering. If you truly can't change the circumstance, what good is obsessing over it? I will insert a frivolous yet important moment here when I took my own advice on this matter. It was my horse's thirtieth birthday, a true milestone, and I looked forward to spending a peaceful morning with him. However, when I arrived at the barn, there was a party on the property, complete with food trucks and lots of children running around. To make matters worse, an ice cream truck soon arrived. I despise the ice cream truck, with its creepy, repetitive music. I have the misfortune of having to listen to it practically every night in my neighborhood, all summer long. I could feel anxiety and anger rise at having our special day ruined. But then I thought, *I can't change it, so I may as well make the best of it!* I led my horse up to the truck and took his birthday picture in front of it. I allowed the children to pet him and answered their questions about how old he was and how long horses live. Now when I hear the ice cream truck, I will remember that special summer day. The term *wu wei* in Taoism is about not manipulating situations that are out of your control. We have to align with the natural ebb and flow of life. I think we can learn a lot from some of the Eastern philosophies.

No matter how dire the situation, suffering comes from wanting things to be different than they are. As the saying goes, *pain is inevitable, but suffering is optional.* I'm not saying you won't grieve over a loss, but healing comes a lot faster if you accept what is. No amount of wishing is going to change it. This circles back to the Buddhist philosophy of nonattachment I mentioned earlier. I admit to being very attached to my things, but I also realize that's my ego speaking and not the light of my soul, who is observing it all. This is not easy for me or for most people—it is an advanced level of human consciousness. This is where it helps to bring the vertical realm of cosmic consciousness (your spirituality or religious beliefs) into awareness and not focus so much on the horizontal timeline of our humanness. Relinquishing some of your ego to let in the light of All That Is will help you see this more clearly. In the end, the entire human aspect of life is reduced to a little horizontal line, the dash that will be on your gravestone between the dates of your birth and death. Regardless of race, gender, age, religion, or political affiliation, everyone's life story is ultimately summed up by a dash. Aren't you so much more than that? You are so much more than a spouse, a parent, a sibling, a son or daughter. You are so much more than an employee in your chosen career. These roles that we identify with are all a part of our horizontal lifeline. Your vertical lifeline is your connection to the eternal. You are the soul that is the awareness of your experience on earth. If you can find alignment where the two crossbars meet, that is the ideal life—make it a balanced and fulfilling one!

Don't let yourself get so entangled in the story inside your head that it consumes you, and you become one of the unconscious ones. Focus on the facts. Be in the *now*, which is all there is. Be more conscious than the majority of society, who are so wrapped up in their closed-minded world of being right about their beliefs on everything from religion and politics to sports and parenting. When your personal story is all you care about, it becomes *your way or the highway*. Wouldn't it be more inclusive to follow the philosophy of *many rays, one sun*? Most of us in the human race are ultimately trying to get to the same end goal (a peaceful death after a well-lived, productive life), but we all take our own unique paths to get there. We are all bit actors in each other's plays. Listen to other points of view. The world (your own stage) will open up to you in astonishing ways when you open your mind. As the spiritual teacher Ram Dass said, *"We are all just walking each other home."*

Consider that everyone gets the same basic 168 hours per week. Divide that into three equal parts, 56 hours each. This is roughly the amount of time the average person spends working, sleeping, and having personal time. Obviously, some of us work more or less and sleep more or less, but let's concentrate on the amount of free time we have. For many of us, this is spent as family time, which can indeed be relaxing and fulfilling, but you also need to carve out some personal time for your own growth and development. If your tank is empty, then you have nothing to share with others. Take a walk in nature and notice all the life around you. Put your phone down, and be mindfully aware of your family, friends, and pets.

The past is all about remembering, and the future is about anticipating. So you might have either regrets or worry that torment your mind. When are you reminiscing about the past? *Now.* When are you worrying about the future? *Now.* Use your five senses to see, hear, feel, taste, and smell your current environment. This is multisensory awareness that only happens in the now. We allegedly have around 60,000 thoughts a day. Mostly this is a repetitive loop of pointless thoughts about the past and future. Life is always a work in progress; our experiences are for the evolution of human consciousness. I'm not asking you to change the consciousness of humanity in general, but think about uplifting those around you that step onto your stage and making a difference in their lives—the ripple effect can be profound.

## CHAPTER 11 TAKEAWAYS

1. What story do you tend to replay in your head (and tell others about) over and over? What is your reason for suffering by repeating the past instead of living in the present?

2. What could you open your mind about to learn something new?

3. What have you suffered from, even while knowing you couldn't change the outcome?

## RESOURCES

* *A New Earth* by Eckhart Tolle
* *The Untethered Soul* by Michael Singer
* *Living Tao: Timeless Principles for Everyday Enlightenment* by Ilchi Lee
* *The Celestine Prophecy* by James Redfield
* *The Alchemist* by Paul Coelho

# CHAPTER 12: YOUR SOUL'S PURPOSE

The timeless intelligence that we call the soul has a purpose here in this earth school. Our job is to discover what that purpose is and align it with our daily lives. Your JOB is Joy Of Being. I'm sure many of you have at least heard of the term *dharma* (rhymes with karma), which basically means your purpose in life. This is where what you love to do and what you're good at triangulate with what the world needs from you. Your career can be a part of your dharma, which would certainly make work more enjoyable, but it isn't all of it. You do not need to monetize your dharma to feel fulfilled and that you are living life to the fullest. Dharma can also evolve over time, but the essence is probably something you've felt since childhood. For example, I've loved horses, dogs, cats, writing, reading, and researching for as long as I can remember. Over time this has evolved into loving and appreciating other species and their specific husbandry needs, integrating holistic medicine and Eastern philosophies into vet medicine and my personal life, and educating clients on the proper care of their individual animals. I've gone from writing fiction to finding a new passion in the nonfiction genre of self-discovery, because this is what I've come to love researching. My love of animals and writing melded with my desire to help others overcome some of the same obstacles I've struggled with, and the idea for this book was born. This is my current dharma.

Everyone has different *archetypes* they identify with, in terms of behavior and psychology. I think many of us in this profession can relate to the Greek mythology centaur Chiron, the wounded healer archetype. He was half human and half animal, a skilled healer, yet wounded physically and emotionally, and he knew what it meant to feel like an outcast. Archetypes can be inherited traits or instincts or something you have chosen to focus on, such as an alter ego. For example, do you consider yourself a healer, teacher, nurturer, or leader? Speaking of leadership, it seems like every clinic expects their licensed veterinary technicians to be leaders these days. While we want to be respected for our education and knowledge in caring for animals, not all of us wish to be leaders of our peers. It can be like shoving a square peg into a round hole, especially if we are highly sensitive or true introverts. Mentoring is different, and I personally enjoy the more relaxed relationship with my teammates. Mentors usually become confidants who offer advice and guidance, whereas leaders don't. I wish more managers would place their staff in roles they are comfortable in, where they can bloom and shine, instead of forcing employees out of their comfort zones to meet some agenda. Micromanaging is one of the surest ways to lose talented personnel. Not everyone needs or wants to be a Chief, and that's okay.

One of the many books I've enjoyed on my journey down the rabbit hole of personal discovery is *The Alter Ego Effect* by Todd Herman. It's about being intentional in which personality needs to show up in different situations to give you more confidence. The superhero persona (also known as an alter ego) can be a real game-changer, along the lines of *fake it until you make it.* Many athletes and celebrities use this tactic of playing a role to get out of the mire of their own heads. Everyone deals with self-doubt, even if only occasionally. Perhaps the most famous example of using an alter ego is how a young gospel singer from Houston, Texas, became a sexy international superstar. Her name is Beyoncé, and her alter ego was Sasha Fierce. While her personal superhero was put on public display onstage, most people choose to keep their alter ego private, a secret boost of confidence, so it can be impactful in a stressful situation. Many athletes have alter egos to help get their heads in the game. They can have completely different personas on and off the arena of their chosen sport. Choose what works for you, whether that is a real person you admire, a fierce animal, a character from a book, or something completely made up. You can have different alter egos for different situations, whether it's playing sports, acting in a play, or standing up to a bully. However, I don't recommend letting others see your Medusa alter ego, as mentioned earlier. Notice how differently children act when they put on a superhero costume. Have fun with this, and watch your courage blossom!

Which form of creativity aligns with your purpose and best flows through you: writing, painting, poetry, building, music, dance? What excites you and puts a bounce in your step? What obstacles have you overcome and perhaps want to help others do the same? And finally, what is the special gift or perspective you bring to the world that makes you unique? This is the special glue, your personal energetic signature, which binds the rest together. Take some time for introspection. When all of these things coalesce, you have found your dharma and are on your way to realizing your full potential.

You may not be familiar with *ikigai* (pronounced icky-guy), the Japanese term that loosely means your reason for getting up in the morning. It's a passion from within that drives your motivation to get things done. It steers you to live with purpose and intention, so you don't let life passively float you downstream to some unknown destination. You have to paddle! (Also known as *God helps those who help themselves.)* This is where action comes in.

A useful lesson in this is the good old-fashioned *vision board.* Typically, you create a vision board by cutting out pictures from magazines of things you want to manifest in your life and making a collage of sorts, to hang where you will see it daily. This unconsciously brings that energy frequency into your life, and bingo, you have a Mercedes in your driveway! Okay, maybe not quite like that. The important key that most don't know is to include pictures of all the hard work it will take to achieve your goals. Align your energetic frequency with what you desire. If you want to run a marathon, just having a picture of a triumphant person crossing the finish line may not be enough to motivate you. You'd better include pictures of people working out, sweating, eating healthy, worn-out sneakers, stopwatches . . . you get the idea. Just having a picture of a person holding a published book wouldn't be enough to keep me on track to write this. But seeing images of sleepless nights, working hard, typing and hand-writing, researching, and a timeline were enough to show me that it would all be worth it in the end. No amount of hoping for a miraculous manifestation was going to write this book for me. Find an accountability partner, and truly be there for each other. Don't be a passenger in your life, and don't settle for mediocrity. Read and do your research on subjects that are in alignment with your best self, but *learn it to live it* and engage by implementing action steps. Just reading about meditating or running a 5K won't actually help you achieve any goals. (Yes, I've done this too.)

## CHAPTER 12 TAKEAWAYS

1. What action steps can you take to realize your dreams of becoming the best version of yourself?

2. Have you discovered your dharma?

3. What is your purpose for getting out of bed in the morning? (Hint: it is not to get your children ready for school.)

4. How would making a vision board help keep your dreams and goals in sight?

5. Who can you count on to hold you accountable? Can you do the same for them?

## RESOURCES

* *Discover Your Dharma* by Sahara Rose
* *The Seat of the Soul* by Gary Zukav
* *The Secret* by Rhonda Byrne
* *Ikigai: Giving Every Day Meaning and Joy* by Yukari Mitsuhashi
* *The Alter Ego Effect* by Todd Herman
* *Big Magic* by Elizabeth Gilbert

# CHAPTER 13: INTEGRATIVE MEDICINE

There are so many healing methods beyond the traditional Western techniques we are taught in this country. If you're working on a difficult case, and things aren't improving, step outside the box and consider reaching out to a holistic vet. Where knowledge ends, frustration begins. Imagine if we saw other vets as collaborative teammates instead of competition! There is a difference between curing and healing, and both have a place. Healing is to come to wholeness on all levels: physical, mental, and spiritual. This idea seems to be gaining traction as energy medicine becomes more popular in mainstream society. While there are more and more critical care and specialty hospitals that we are comfortable sending patients to (cardiac, oncology, internal medicine, neurology, ophthalmology, etc.), don't forget integrative medicine. Traditional Chinese Veterinary Medicine (TCVM) is an amazing but complicated modality that encompasses acupuncture, food therapy, herbal medicine, and *tui na* (a form of massage known as Chinese medical manipulation). I took the vet tech course offered by the Chi Institute in Florida, and it opened up a whole new understanding of healing. I personally know of several dogs that were given many more years of life because their caretakers were willing to try acupuncture. For some it was a last resort before euthanasia (I don't recommend waiting that long).

Energy medicine is another route to healing and relieving stress, and the world is awakening to it as it becomes more mainstream. Energetic vibration is the essence of what animates every living thing, and I believe it is the next frontier in healing. While there are still many skeptics, it makes sense that if our physical bodies are made up of energy, then treating that aspect will help heal the physical part. Look up Dr. Masaru Emoto's water consciousness experiment for a mind-blowing look at how energy changes water molecules.

It was one of my best bosses who started me on the journey of exploring the energy medicine modality in 2008. Although he was of an older generation and talking about retirement at the time I was hired, he was progressive and open-minded about the future of veterinary medicine. I worked for him for eleven years, and he was one of the few bosses who was never disrespectful or condescending toward me. He knew about my interest in holistic medicine, and even though it wasn't something we offered at the practice, he sent me to a course on *Healing Touch For Animals (HTA)*. It's an understatement to say that it changed the trajectory of my life. That course was taught by the founder of HTA, Carol Komitor, who was visiting from Colorado. I took two more courses with her, advancing up the levels. I witnessed a myriad of ways in which an invisible energy frequency can support the body in healing itself. In a nutshell, this life-force energy is channeled through the practitioner and into the animal. An energetically balanced body is then able to relax to allow the self-healing process to work. When the physical body is relaxed, there is a cascade of effects: endorphin release, increased circulation, better nutrient absorption, increased oxygen in the blood, and a release of toxin buildup, to name a few. It's not unlike the effects of massage, but the recipient doesn't even need to be touched, and in fact, distance healing works just as well as in person. What I witnessed blew my mind. It was yet another boss who sent me to the Chi Institute to learn TCVM—I was hooked and eager to learn more.

Several students in the HTA classes also practiced a modality called *Reiki* (pronounced ray-key). Around that time, my brother mentioned that he recently had a session, and I found it interesting, but the only thing I knew was how to spell the word. I went to the bookstore, bought a copy of *Reiki News* magazine, and found a Level 1 and 2 class being taught a few hours away. Reiki is life-force energy channeled from the Source of all consciousness (many call this God), through the practitioner's hands, and into the human, animal, or plant being treated. Energy is not confined by any religious dogma—anything with a life force can be treated successfully. It is similar to HTA in its delivery, but it has its own frequency and is passed down from Source to the practitioner in a sacred ceremony. Think of distance Reiki like prayer, in that it can bridge any distance to support those in need. This can be explained by quantum physics, which is clearly beyond the scope of this book. Keep in mind that unlike prayer, Reiki practitioners should be paid for their services, as they have been specially trained in channeling the energy. It can be awkward when someone says, "Hey, can you send Reiki to my aunt in the hospital?" and you have to ask for payment. Be respectful that this is a profession, with a lot of time and education invested. Payment doesn't have to be an exchange of currency, and in fact can include an exchange of energy such as the bartering system, as long as you give something back or pay it forward in a mutual agreement.

I delved into the lifestyle and worked my way up through the levels over the next decade. I earned my Reiki Master Practitioner certification on my brother's birthday, which made me proud, as he was one of the first to bring this modality to my attention. I've also taken Rainbow Reiki, which is a more relaxed and shamanistic practice. I went on a Reiki retreat to Sedona, Arizona, and had the time of my life. The first word that popped into my head when I saw those majestic red rock formations was *home,* even though I'd never been there before. Although I went on this trip solo, I met many wonderful people who will forever be a part of my life. I fell so in love with Sedona that I went back, again alone, two years later for my Karuna Reiki Master course. Karuna is an advanced yet gentle frequency of Reiki, which radiates compassion and facilitates healing at a cellular level. Although all the classes I've attended were taught on humans, I've mostly practiced on animals, as that is my calling. Finally, there is an official Animal Reiki course within the Usui system that I follow (the International Center for Reiki Training) that was years in the making, which I completed in the spring of 2021. Reiki is practiced at hundreds of human hospitals around the world, where it reduces pain and speeds healing time. All you have to do is ask for a practitioner if you're having a procedure. Reiki is one of the top three complementary therapies being offered in hospitals, after massage and music therapy. It is slowly catching on in animal hospitals and is more widely utilized in shelters, where it can have a profound effect on reducing stress.

At yet another closed-minded clinic (I sure can find them, can't I?), I was told by the manager and one doctor that I couldn't call myself an energy healer, as was stated on my business cards. They said it "just isn't true," although they knew absolutely nothing about what I do and never cared to ask. I just had to laugh and shake my head at their ignorance, because I've spent thousands of dollars and earned many certificates over the last decade, indicating that I indeed have the ability to channel healing energy, just like thousands of other people. Let me be clear: we do not perform any healing, we are simply the vessel for energy to pass through, so the body can facilitate its own healing. I didn't last long at that clinic, but there was a silver lining in that one person believed in me and became a good friend. She eventually left as well, and we were reunited at another clinic, where we still work together. I truly believe in synchronicity and that things happen for a reason. I can't count the number of wonderful, hardworking employees who have left vet clinics due to poor management with big egos and no people skills. Shame on the owners of these practices for not listening and intervening.

I am blessed that the practice I currently work for, and hope to remain at until I retire, is open-minded and strives to have an inclusive culture. A relief vet, two licensed techs, and the manager all practice Reiki. Another vet there does acupuncture, a form of complementary medicine that uses energy meridians in the body. I still get made fun of at times, like being called a hippie, but it's all in good fun. Several staff members also carry crystals in their pockets or wear them as necklaces. It's a completely different atmosphere when you finally find your tribe. Don't stop searching until you find yours.

Animal Reiki is practiced differently than human Reiki. With most people, we can get verbal or written consent, and there is typically a set routine of hand positions that we follow. With Animal Reiki, we need to get consent from the caretaker and then from the animal itself. Sometimes they will tell you in no uncertain terms that they want no part of this. Other times, animals gladly soak up the energy like a sponge (especially cats and horses, who have a special affinity for it). If the animal is stray or wild, you must ask permission from them as well. If they move away or you are able to hear a "No" in your head, you must respect that. Although Reiki cannot harm, it is their right to choose their own destiny. Let them move in and out of the energy field of their own free will. Animals are far more in tune with energy than most humans. We think too much and analyze everything, but they just enjoy it in the moment. One experience I won't soon forget was when I was practicing a technique for a case study for an online class. I still get skeptical and have self-doubt, and I remember thinking *I doubt this will work* as I entered an exam room, where a large-breed dog was spending a few days medical boarding with us. Both of her knees needed surgery, and it was excruciating to watch her try to stand and walk. As I entered the room, she was panting and pacing, her knees wobbling. Although she was on several pain medications, she was obviously uncomfortable. I sat on the floor, crossed my legs, and meditated. I imagined the healing Reiki energy flowing out of my hands and surrounding me. The next thing I knew, that dog had backed up to literally sit in my lap, so my hands could easily rest on her knees. She sat there for a good amount of time, and in the photo a coworker took, I swear she was smiling. When she'd had enough, she went to lay down and promptly fell asleep—I believe it was the best rest she'd had in days. It was a lesson in trusting the energy and allowing the animal to make its own decision. I still see her from time to time, and she is doing very well after her surgeries.

As much as I love energy healing, I don't always feel tingling or heat in my hands, as many others do. I don't get messages in my head or see angels or colors—yet. For a long time, I felt like a failure and was told by a classmate to stop being negative. I wasn't trying to be negative at all—I was simply stating my personal reality. I'm not going to pretend or make up stories to fit in. This happened to me in an Animal Communication course as well. Out of about twenty-five participants, I'm pretty sure I was the only one whose mind was blank—not one animal came through for me. Honestly, I think I want things so badly sometimes that I unconsciously block my own progress—my ego gets in the way. One girl was crying because her horse that had been dead for twenty years came through to give her a message. Others were communicating with nature spirits in the surrounding woods. I was looking at a Golden Retriever and thinking *Well, he's probably friendly. I'm sure he carries his leash in his mouth and loves to play with toys.* I truly believe there are people who communicate with animals; I've heard some amazing stories from credible witnesses. I just don't happen to be one of them at this time in my development, and that's okay. (So much for my plan to be Super Tech: "Hey, he says it's his pancreas that's the problem!" Sigh.) I have come to understand that Reiki works no matter what, and that my senses work more with *claircognizance* (intuitive knowledge) than *clairtangency* (knowing by touching). The people or animals I am working on definitely feel something, even when I don't. My boss's daughter had an athletic injury, and she told me the energy felt like "warm spiders" (not the most ringing endorsement, but I understood what she meant and grinned from ear to ear). The energy goes where it is needed, as it is divinely guided by a source much more intelligent than we are. My job is simply to let it flow through me to help our pets be energetically as well as physically healed.

My geriatric horse receives Reiki regularly, both in person and distantly. In fact, he seems to find great relief when he receives it, licking and yawning dozens of times in a row before taking a nap. (These behaviors demonstrate ways in which equines release physical and emotional tension.) He seems to enjoy Reiki more than massage, which I can understand at his age. I know that when it is finally his time to gallop across the Rainbow Bridge, he will do so wrapped in the flow of loving, healing energy. I now regularly channel Reiki to every euthanasia I attend—it is my parting gift to them.

I know beyond a doubt that energy healing works, and I have my own special gifts to share. You don't have to be a Reiki practitioner to utilize the Reiki Ideals, which can keep you centered and focused on the positive throughout the day. Set your intention to focus on at least one of the following:

1. Just for today, do not worry.
2. Just for today, do not anger.
3. Just for today, work diligently.
4. Just for today, be thankful and show gratitude.
5. Just for today, be kind to others.

Even though you may not understand how something works, be open-minded and give it a try. Ask questions and do research. Some of these methods have been around for thousands of years—they would have died off long ago if there were no success stories. I can vouch for acupuncture on myself as well. I've had two instances (tennis elbow and a pinched nerve with numb fingers) where my general practitioner and chiropractor could no longer help me. I was in pain for weeks before trying acupuncture. Each time, I was completely healed in two sessions. I now turn to complementary medicine as my first line of defense in most instances and certainly for chronic problems. Western medicine is still considered best for acute cases or emergencies. However, don't disregard other additions, such as massage, chiropractic, essential oils (plant energy), CBD, supplements, and high-quality "living" nutrition. I see so many vets roll their eyes and immediately negate these modalities, which they admittedly know nothing about. Knowing that there are options available other than pharmaceuticals for our patients can alleviate some of the stress of treating them.

## CHAPTER 13 TAKEAWAYS

1. What are your special gifts to share with the world?

2. Do you believe in energy healing? Why or why not? Is it a personal, religious, or cultural belief?

3. Would you be open to using energy healing or TCVM in your practice as a complementary therapy or at least sharing a case with a holistic vet?

4. Which of the Reiki Ideals do you find the easiest to implement during your day?

## RESOURCES

* www.reiki.org
* www.reikilifestyle.com
* www.shelteranimalreikiassociation.org
* www.animalreikisource.com
* www.ahvma.org
* www.tcvm.com and www.tcvmherbal.com
* *Everything Animal Reiki: A Simple Guide to Meditating with Animals for Healing* by Kathleen Prasad
* *Heart to Heart with Horses: The Equine Lover's Guide to Reiki* by Kathleen Prasad
* *Vets on Animal Reiki: The Power of Animal Reiki Healing in Veterinary Practice* by Kathleen Prasad
* *The Hidden Messages in Water* by Dr. Masaru Emoto
* *The Call of Sedona: Journey of the Heart* by Ilchi Lee
* *Four Paws, Five Directions* by Cheryl Schwartz, DVM
* *Eastern Body, Western Mind* by Anodea Judith

# FINAL THOUGHTS AND ACTION STEPS

It is my sincere hope that you learned some new techniques and tools to help you cope with the hardships of veterinary medicine—or any career or relationship. If any of the resources I have mentioned resonate with you, please do your own further research. Stand tall in your truth, be kind to others, and take the high road when possible (there's not much traffic). Meet people where they are. We are all on different paths, and each one is uniquely ordered just for us. Respect that and have compassion, while not letting your spirit get stomped on. Stand up to bullies, as no one has the right to tread on your personal path without invitation.

Challenge yourself to a thirty-day happiness makeover. Try a new, small habit every week, and build upon it until it becomes routine. Don't get rid of an old habit without replacing it with something better, or it will leave a void. Read some new books, listen to uplifting podcasts, and download meditation apps. Make your inner experience the best it can be, and it will shine through and mend those cracks in your foundation, allowing you to shed joy and light to those around you.

**Week 1:** Be mindful of your self-deprecating thoughts or judgments. As soon as you are aware, replace them with more positive ones. Repeat your affirmations to yourself. You are good at this! You are enough!

**Week 2:** Now that you're clearing up your mental clutter, move on to your office or house, and work on eliminating physical clutter. Get rid of those items that don't bring you joy. Start small until you see a difference—this will build momentum.

**Week 3:** Focus on avoiding sugary carbs at work. When you feel stressed, meditate for a few minutes, and remind yourself that your body needs nourishment, not garbage. Bring healthy options to work.

**Week 4:** Implement small things that can change the culture of your working environment. If you're the boss, what can you do to show appreciation for your staff? How can you treat them more kindly and ensure their happiness in their allotted roles? If you're an employee, how can you raise the vibration of your coworkers to a positive one? Do this consistently, and we can all make a difference and perhaps even save a life that was in jeopardy. You just never know the impact you can make.

Start living proactively and with purpose. Practice new habits *until.* There are no deadlines or overnight successes—just a lot of hard work behind the scenes, but it's worth the investment in yourself. Start over as many times as you need to. Just don't give up on your quest to lead a more peaceful, purposeful, and joyful life! Day 1 is always better than "One day . . ."

# ACKNOWLEDGMENTS

First and foremost, I would like to thank my parents for giving me both the roots to ground me and the wings to fly as high as I chose. Raising a highly sensitive child was not always an easy road. I know that the gifts of criticism and advice always come wrapped in love. They have supported me in more ways than I can ever thank them for. They may grumble about any new pet I welcome home, but that is soon followed by an unwavering love for them as well.

Thank you to everyone who has ever read one of my manuscripts and encouraged my passion for writing. Your words of encouragement kept me on this path to become an author. I'm sorry it took so long to see one of my books make it out of my head and into the light of day. A heartfelt thank-you to my coworkers and friends who took the time to read and honestly edit and critique several drafts of this book: Jacie Dannhardt, Shayna Swanson, Jan Schlesinger, Theresa Thompson, and Leslie Hearn. Thank you to the team at Self-Publishing School: my coach Ellaine, my editor and formatter Robin L. Reed, and my cover designer. You all were the kick in the butt that I needed to be held accountable in making my dream a reality.

The books and teachings of the following people have inspired me over the years to be the best version of myself: Oprah Winfrey, Eckhart Tolle, Dr. Phil McGraw, Mel Robbins, and Hal Elrod. They have been my mentors from afar.

Thank you to my respectful bosses and coworkers over the years, many of whom are dear friends. One of my favorite former bosses was kind enough to write the foreword to this book, for which I am grateful. Several of you have shared your personal struggles with me, and I thank you for letting me use your stories to help others. To those who hurled lemons at me, know that this book is my sweet lemonade. I hope that you open your minds and hearts to the way you treat people and the repercussions it can have.

Last but far from least, a special thank-you to all the animals in my life, past and present, personal and professional. Without their unconditional love, I wouldn't have made it through some of the darker days with such strength. They have taught me so much about life and love, patience and perseverance. They are my joy and reason for being.

# ABOUT THE AUTHOR

Tracy has been an advocate for animals her whole life, and more recently, an advocate for those working tirelessly on the front lines caring for them. She has an Associate's degree from the State University of New York at Delhi in Veterinary Science Technology and a Bachelor's degree in Equine Science from Colorado State University. Although Tracy is a traditionally trained, licensed veterinary technician with over thirty years of experience, she has a special interest in integrative medicine. She started her own energy healing and pet sitting company, Wind Moon Wellness, LLC, in 2010. She is a Holy Fire III Karuna Reiki Master, a Certified Equine Sports Massage Therapist, and a Certified Professional Pet Sitter. Tracy has also been trained in Traditional Chinese Veterinary Medicine and therapeutic-grade essential oils for animals. Her first passion will always be horses, but she currently shares her Virginia home with three sighthounds, several cats and geckos, a bearded dragon, a guinea pig, three parrots, and a few rats. Her equine partner, Harley, resides nearby.

Printed in Great Britain
by Amazon

12950918R00081